Capital Punishment

Other books in the Social Issues Firsthand series:

SOCIAL ISSUES
FIRSTHAND

Capital Punishment

Steffanie Richardson, Book Editor

GREENHAVEN PRESS

An imprint of Thomson Gale, a part of The Thomson Corporation

THOMSON

GALE

Detroit • New York • San Francisco • New Haven, Conn. • Waterville, Maine • London • Munich

Bonnie Szumski, *Publisher*
Helen Cothran, *Managing Editor*
Scott Barbour, *Series Editor*

LIBRARY OF CONGRESS CATALOGING-IN-PUBLICATION DATA

Capital punishment / Steffanie Richardson, book editor
  p. cm. -- (Social issues firsthand)
  Includes bibliographical references and index.
  0-7377-2496-X (lib. : alk. paper)
  1. Capital punishment--United States. 2. Death row--United States.
  3. Death row inmates--United States. I. Richardson, Steffanie. II. Series.
  HV8699.U5C2926 2006
  364.660973--dc22

                                                        2006041074

Printed in the United States of America
10 9 8 7 6 5 4 3 2 1

Contents

Chapter 1: Perspectives of Death Row Inmates

Chapter 2: Views of Participants in the Death Penalty

Chapter 3: Voices of Families Touched by the Death Penalty

Foreword

Social issues are often viewed in abstract terms. Pressing challenges such as poverty, homelessness, and addiction are viewed as problems to be defined and solved. Politicians, social scientists, and other experts engage in debates about the extent of the problems, their causes, and how best to remedy them. Often overlooked in these discussions is the human dimension of the issue. Behind every policy debate over poverty, homelessness, and substance abuse, for example, are real people struggling to make ends meet, to survive life on the streets, and to overcome addiction to drugs and alcohol. Their stories are ubiquitous and compelling. They are the stories of everyday people—perhaps your own family members or friends—and yet they rarely influence the debates taking place in state capitols, the national Congress, or the courts.

The disparity between the public debate and private experience of social issues is well illustrated by looking at the topic of poverty. Each year the U.S. Census Bureau establishes a poverty threshold. A household with an income below the threshold is defined as poor, while a household with an income above the threshold is considered able to live on a basic subsistence level. For example, in 2003 a family of two was considered poor if its income was less than $12,015; a family of four was defined as poor if its income was less than $18,810. Based on this system, the bureau estimates that 35.9 million Americans (12.5 percent of the population) lived below the poverty line in 2003, including 12.9 million children below the age of eighteen.

Commentators disagree about what these statistics mean. Social activists insist that the huge number of officially poor Americans translates into human suffering. Even many families that have incomes above the threshold, they maintain, are likely to be struggling to get by. Other commentators insist that the statistics exaggerate the problem of poverty in the United States. Compared to people in developing countries, they point out, most so-called poor families have a high quality of life. As stated by journalist Fidelis Iyebote, "Cars are owned by 70 percent of 'poor' households. . . . Color televisions belong to 97 percent of the 'poor' [and] videocassette recorders belong to nearly 75 percent. . . . Sixty-four percent have microwave ovens, half own a stereo system, and over a quarter possess an automatic dishwasher."

However, this debate over the poverty threshold and what it means is likely irrelevant to a person living in poverty. Simply put, poor people do not need the government to tell them whether they are poor. They can see it in the stack of bills they cannot pay. They are aware of it when they are forced to choose between paying rent or buying food for their children. They become painfully conscious of it when they lose their homes and are forced to live in their cars or on the streets. Indeed, the written stories of poor people define the meaning of poverty more vividly than a government bureaucracy could ever hope to. Narratives composed by the poor describe losing jobs due to injury or mental illness, depict horrific tales of childhood abuse and spousal violence, recount the loss of friends and family members. They evoke the slipping away of social supports and government assistance, the descent into substance abuse and addiction, the harsh realities of life on the streets. These are the perspectives on poverty that are too often omitted from discussions over the extent of the problem and how to solve it.

Greenhaven Press's Social Issues Firsthand series provides a forum for the often-overlooked human perspectives on society's most divisive topics of debate. Each volume focuses on one social issue and presents a collection of ten to sixteen narratives by those who have had personal involvement with the topic. Extra care has been taken to include a diverse range of perspectives. For example, in the volume on adoption, readers will find the stories of birth parents who have made an adoption plan, adoptive parents, and adoptees themselves. After exposure to these varied points of view, the reader will have a clearer understanding that adoption is an intense, emotional experience full of joyous highs and painful lows for all concerned.

The debate surrounding embryonic stem cell research illustrates the moral and ethical pressure that the public brings to bear on the scientific community. However, while nonexperts often criticize scientists for not considering the potential negative impact of their work, ironically the public's reaction against such discoveries can produce harmful results as well. For example, although the outcry against embryonic stem cell research in the United States has resulted in fewer embryos being destroyed, those with Parkinson's, such as actor Michael J. Fox, have argued that prohibiting the development of new stem cell lines ultimately will prevent a timely cure for the disease that is killing Fox and thousands of others.

Each book in the series contains several features that enhance its usefulness, including an in-depth introduction, an annotated table of contents, bibliographies for further research, a list of organizations to contact, and a thorough index. These elements—combined with the poignant voices of people touched by tragedy and triumph—make the Social Issues Firsthand series a valuable resource for research on today's topics of political discussion.

Introduction

Capital punishment is the most severe criminal penalty used in the United States. It is reserved for only the most heinous instances of the most serious crime: murder. Because the sentence involves the taking of a life, the government does not rush to carry it out. Instead, the convict undergoes a lengthy appeals process that typically lasts years, even decades. This process, which is intended to ensure that only the truly guilty are put to death, often leads to a drawn out period of torment for the convict who languishes on death row waiting for the inevitable end to come. It can also add to the suffering of the murder victims' families, who in turn find themselves in a state of limbo as they grapple with their desire for retribution and closure.

Lingering on Death Row

Almost every state's death penalty statute requires an automatic review of all death sentences by the state supreme court. If a death sentence is upheld by the state supreme court, the defendant may appeal to the U.S. Supreme Court. If the Court refuses to vacate the death penalty, then the defendant may still slow the process by initiating habeas corpus proceedings based on any legal issue that might not previously have been considered. Because of all these appeals an inmate can potentially spend decades awaiting execution.

While this extra time may seem to benefit the inmate by safeguarding against wrongful executions, the Court has found that extended times between sentencing and execution often result in "immense mental anxiety amounting to a great increase in the offender's punishment."[1] This finding has given rise to growing sentiment among anti–death penalty advocates that forcing prisoners to linger on death row directly violates their Eighth Amendment protection against cruel and unusual punishment. Usually remaining in their cells for as many as twenty-three hours a day, death row inmates are often isolated from other prisoners and excluded from prison employment and educational programs. In addition, their outdoor exercise and personal visitation privileges are extremely limited.

Studies have found that living in this extended solitary confinement, coupled with the drawn out appeals process, can leave prisoners with psychological damage that is likened to the sufferings of prisoners of war or victims of torture. Stuart Grassian, a Harvard Medical School psychiatrist and one of the country's leading specialists on death row inmates, contends that this kind of isolation is "toxic to mental functioning"[2] and affects the ability to focus attention or to shift attention. The end result is often permanent mental damage. Grassian and others conclude that due to the suffering death row inmates experience, the death penalty constitutes two sentences: the death sentence itself and the punishment of living in a constant state of isolation and uncertainty regarding the date of execution. As Grassian explains: "The conditions of confinement are so oppressive, the helplessness endured in the roller coaster of hope and despair so wrenching and exhausting, that ultimately the inmate can no longer bear it, and then it is only in dropping his appeals that he has any sense of control over his fate."[3]

An example of an inmate who chose to drop his appeals process is Michael Ross, who was executed on May 13, 2005. Ross was the first man to be executed in Connecticut in forty-five years. Prior to his execution he attested that the isolation he felt while on death row thinking about his crimes and his impending lethal injection caused him to waive any appeals so that he could "end his own pain." He describes his eighteen-year stay on death row:

> I had absolutely no privacy. I got dressed in front of the guard. I used the toilet in front of the guard. Everything that I did was in front of the guard. You cannot begin to imagine

what that absolute and total lack of privacy does to you. You cannot begin to imagine how it begins to destroy your very sense of humanity—like you are an animal in a cage on display at the zoo. No wonder I spiraled into a clinical depression and had visions of my own execution.[4]

Of course, many people, especially pro-death penalty advocates, are disinclined to sympathize with the suffering of death row inmates. They insist that murderers have waived their right to live an easy life by denying their victims any rights at all. After all, those who are sentenced to death have committed murder with special circumstances, such as murder for financial gain, murder with torture, or murder of a police officer on duty. They have been found guilty of the most vicious crimes imaginable. Advocates for the victims, including the families of many victims, reject the assertion that death row inmates are subjected to excessive punishment. Author David Anderson echoes the sentiments of many who do not feel that the government is required to provide leniency to a murderer:

> The violent criminal and murderer do not deserve the compassion of the state governed by law. One who in the most heinous way lacks to show compassion towards fellow men does not have an obvious right to expect the compassion of the state governed by law. As soon as the word compassion is mentioned we need to turn our attention to the victim and his relatives.[5]

Death as a Means of Closure

The long appeals process for death penalty cases not only affects the inmates; it also impacts the families of their victims. Families of murder victims vary in their attitudes toward the murderer of their loved ones. Some believe the murderer's death will bring a sense of justice and personal closure; others want execution but also want to forgive the murderer. Still others may oppose death for the killer and choose complete

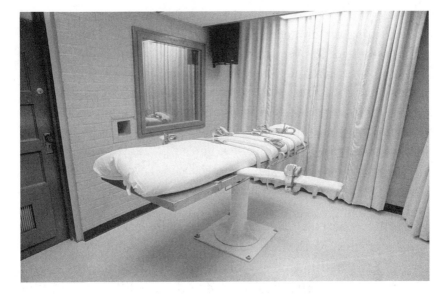

Lethal injection is the most widely used method of execution in the United States. This is the lethal injection room at the Huntsville, Texas prison. © Greg Smith/CORBIS

forgiveness as their path to healing. Regardless of their personal philosophy toward the death penalty, all families of murder victims must cope with the long wait for the resolution of the death penalty sentence. For many, the lengthy process adds to the grief and lack of closure that is inevitable when a loved one is suddenly, violently taken away. To some, the long delay merely compounds the injustice done to their family member.

Joshua Ryen has been waiting for retribution since the 1983 murder of his family and childhood friend. As the only survivor of the multiple murders, Ryen has been forced to linger just as his family's murderer, Kevin Cooper, has lingered on death row. Ryen wants the kind of closure that he feels the death penalty will afford him, but the appeals process has continued to stay Cooper's execution. In this excerpt from a 2004 statement, Ryen urges the court to finish the punishment that it mandated for Cooper in 1985:

Every time Cooper claims he's innocent and sends people scurrying off on another wild goose chase I have to relive the murders all over again. It runs like a horror movie, over and over again and never stops because he never shuts up. He puts PR [public relations] people on national television who say outrageous things and then the press wants to know what I think. What I think is that I would like to be rid of Kevin Cooper. I would like for him to go away. I would like to never hear from Kevin Cooper again. I would like Kevin Cooper to pay for what he did.[6]

Some experts caution that seeking the culprit's death as a means of closure can ultimately leave family members dissatisfied. Lula Redmond, a Florida therapist who works with victims' families, says, "Taking a life doesn't fill that void. But it's generally not until after the execution [that the families] realize this. Not too many people will honestly [say] publicly that it didn't do much, though, because they've spent most of their lives trying to get someone to the death chamber."[7]

Other family members seek closure by forgiving the killer of their loved one. It is commonly thought that forgiveness means letting go of all blame, even relieving the killer of accountability for the crime. However, according to the International Forgiveness Institute, a private nonprofit organization whose goal is to implement forgiveness as a means to personal and societal health, forgiveness is defined as "the foregoing of resentment or revenge when the wrongdoer's actions deserve it and giving the gifts of mercy, generosity and love when the wrongdoer does not deserve them."[8]

Bill Pelke is one survivor who chose to forgive rather than seek closure through the death penalty. In 1985 four teenage girls murdered his grandmother. He has since devoted his life to the abolition of the death penalty. "The death penalty has absolutely nothing to do with healing," Pelke states. "[It] just continues the cycle of violence and creates more murder victim's family members. We become what we hate. We become killers."[9]

While each survivor finds peace in his or her own way, the commonality lies in the need for closure. But closure is difficult to find after a crime that leaves so much pain in its wake. The narratives in this volume serve to illustrate the principle that the effects of one action are rarely isolated. Like a stone thrown into a pond, the death penalty touches not only those immediately involved; its ripples have far-reaching effects that can take years to be seen.

Notes

1. U.S. Supreme Court, *Foster v. Florida*, 2002.
2. Quoted in Claire Schaeffer-Duffy, "Long Term Lockdown," *National Catholic Reporter*, December 8, 2000.
3. Quoted in "Time on Death Row," 2006. www.deathpenaltyinfo.org.
4. Michael Ross, "Why I Chose to Die Rather than to Fight for Life," Canadian Coalition Against the Death Penalty, April 2005. www.ccdap.org.
5. David Anderson, *The Death Penalty: A Defense*, 2005. www.yesdeathpenalty.com.
6. Quoted in *Inland Valley (California) Daily Bulletin*, April 23, 2005.
7. Quoted in "A Place for Vengeance," *U.S. News and World Report*, June 17, 1997.
8. Quoted in "About Forgiveness," Forgiveness Institute. www.forgivenessinstitute. org.
9. Bill Pelke, *Journey of Hope . . . from Violence to Healing*. Journey of Hope, 2004. www.journeyofhope.org.

Perspectives of Death Row Inmates

Execution Can Never Be Humane

Robert Murray

On May 14, 1991, Robert Murray and his brother Roger entered an Arizona home and forced Dean Morrison and Jackie Appel- hans to lie side by side on the floor before shooting them with pistols and a shotgun. The next morning a highway patrol officer attempted to pull the brothers over, but instead the two men led police on a high-speed chase before they finally surrendered to law enforcement. Robert and Roger maintain their innocence as they sit on death row for two counts of first degree murder.

In October 1992, before the brothers arrived on Arizona's death row, Donald Eugene Harding entered Arizona's gas cham- ber and was strapped to a chair. Something went wrong with the execution, causing Harding's body to spasm violently until he died eleven minutes later. Witnesses were appalled at the suffer- ing that Harding appeared to endure. KTVK-TV reporter Cam- eron Harper said, "It was an ugly event. We put animals to death more humanely. This was not a clean and simple death." Arizona's citizens were outraged and sought a more palatable choice for their state's execution system. Lethal injection was pro- posed as a more humane alternative. In response, a new law was passed declaring that anyone sentenced to death prior to Novem- ber 23, 1992, could now choose either the gas chamber or lethal injection. Anyone sentenced after that date is to be executed by lethal injection only.

Because he was sentenced prior to November 23, 1992, Rob- ert Murray was given the choice of how to die. In the following selection Robert writes that this choice is too difficult to make. He describes the arduous death offered by the gas chamber, and then goes on to compare the anguish of waiting for lethal injec-

tion with the mental anxiety of knowing that you are about to be thrown out of a plane. His ultimate conclusion is that there is no humane way to end a life.

Robert Murray also has written the book Life on Death Row, which offers a glimpse into the realities of life, and death, on "the row." Robert's execution has since been stayed.

Execution Can Never Be Humane

The idea of death and dying is never far from my mind. Before coming to death row, I hadn't given much thought to my own demise. I've come very close to death a couple of times, but they were mere moments.

Now not only does the state of Arizona intend to kill me; they want me to participate in the process by deciding the method they will use. It's a strange form of polite behavior. For years, state officials have determined every aspect of my existence. Now, in a sudden burst of good manners, they want to add a bit of civility to my death by offering me a choice.

They've given me 2 methods to consider: lethal injection and lethal gas. I often imagine myself in the gas chamber and try to guess at the difference between dying there and dying by lethal injection. But I just keep coming back to the outcome. I wanted to ask someone's advice about which method I should choose, but dead is dead, and the handful of people I might have consulted are testaments to this finality.

The Easy Way to Die

Lethal injection is now paraded about as the easy way to die. Most of the public is under the impression that since lethal injection seems simple and painless it somehow makes killing more acceptable. Witnesses to injection executions come away with the illusory perception that a patient has fallen asleep. Typical witnesss testimony goes something like this: "Well, he just seemed to fall asleep."

"Could you better describe the event?"

"We were standing there, and suddenly the curtain opened and there he was, just lying there."

"What happened next?"

"Well, like I said, he was just lying there looking at the ceiling. His lips were moving a little, and he . . . well, you know, he just closed his eyes and went to sleep. I wasn't expecting it to be so easy and fast. He just went to sleep."

Easy as going to sleep. I have thought about this for literally hundreds of hours. Easy as falling asleep. I guess everybody wants to die as easily as they fall asleep.

The state of Arizona has given me a description of the 2 methods of execution from which I am allowed to choose:

One (1) pound of sodium cyanide is placed in a container underneath the gas chamber chair. The chair is made of perforated metal which allows the cyanide gas to pass through and fill the chamber. A bowl below the chair contains sulfuric acid and distilled water. A lever is pulled and the sodium cyanide falls into the solution, releasing the gas. It takes the prisoner several minutes to die. After the execution, the excess gas is released through an exhaust pipe which extends about 50 feet above the Death House.

Inmates executed by lethal injection are brought into the injection room a few minutes prior to the appointed time of execution. He/she is then strapped to a gurney-type bed and two (2) sets of intravenous tubes are inserted, one (1) in each arm. The three (3) drugs used include: sodium pentothal (a sedative intended to put the inmate to sleep); Pavulon (stops breathing and paralyzes the muscular system); and Potassium Chloride (causes the heart to stop). Death by lethal injection is not painful and the inmate goes to sleep prior to the fatal effects of the Pavulon and Potassium Chloride.

These descriptions do not begin to illustrate the overall reality of an injection. The claim "Death by lethal injection is not painful . . ." is far from accurate, and "going to sleep" with an overdose of sodium pentothal isn't all it's cracked up to be. It's death by any definition. The pain lies in the years, months, days, hours, minutes, and seconds leading up to the moment of execution. The pain lies in choosing your own method of execution. Going to sleep while strapped to a table is the least of it; in fact, it ends a great deal of pain—the terror, nightmares, and constant internal struggles.

Is Any Execution Humane?

The gas chamber was introduced to Arizona in the 1930s. Before that, the state hanged people. Nooses from every execution were saved and displayed in glass cases on the walls of the witness chamber of the death house. Hanging was discontinued after a woman was accidentally decapitated in 1930.

On April 6, 1992, at 12:18 A.M., Donald Harding was pronounced dead after spending a full 11 minutes in the state's gas chamber. It was Arizona's 1st execution in 29 years, and state officials were somewhat out of practice. The spectacle of Harding gasping in the execution chamber was a little too hard for people to handle. In response, a movement grew to make executions more "humane."

Suddenly there was a new political crisis. People were outraged. Politicians took to the stump. State execution was cruel, ghastly, horrid. It took a prisoner 11 minutes to cough up his life to the gas. Of course, if executions could be made to seem more humane, that was something else altogether.

It was a wonderful political banner to wave come election time: Arizona would continue to execute people, but they would be 'nice' executions. The politicians went about their task with glee. They preserved their rights to kill people by coming up with a new way to kill people. Lethal injection was their new champion, and champion it they did.

Several months after Harding's execution, a new law was born: "Any person sentenced to death prior to November 23,

1992, is afforded a choice of execution by either lethal gas or lethal injection. Inmates receiving death after November 23, 1992, are to be executed by lethal injection."

As it happened, my brother Roger and I were sentenced to death on October 26, 1992. We were among the lucky few who were given a Hobson's choice about how we should die.

Offering prisoners a "humane" execution seems to be the latest strategy to keep capital punishment alive. But the notion that any execution could be humane eludes me. People today seem generally happy with the idea of lethal injection, as long as it is done in a neat, sanitary, easy-to-watch fashion. I'm not sure what this says about our society. However, I am sure most people don't grasp the reality of the "sleeping" death of which they so widely approve. Indeed, many witnesses leave an execution with a serene look on their faces, as if they'd just seen a somewhat pleasant movie. To my mind, it's actually the witnesses who are falling asleep at injection killings, lulled by the calmness of it all.

Emotions Felt Prior to Execution

As I see it, death by injection is very like being tossed out of an airplane. Supose I'm told that on November 3, someone will escort me from my cell, take me up in an airplane, and, at 3:00 in the afternoon, toss me out without a parachute. After a few minutes, my body will hit a target area, killing me immediately. It's an easy, instant, painless death. The impact of hitting the ground after falling several thousand feet will kill me as instantly and effectively as lethal injection.

Killing inmates by tossing them out of airplanes would of course be unacceptable to the public. But why? It's as fast and effective as lethal injection. The terror of falling 2 minutes isn't all that different from the terror of lying strapped to a table, and neither is physically painful. There's a similar waiting process before each execution. If an airplane is used, you wait for the time it takes the aircraft to take off and reach the target area at the proper altitude. For lethal injection, you wait in the death house until everything's ready and all possibility of a stay of execution has been exhausted. In an airplane, a cargo door is opened; in the death house, a curtain across the viewing window is drawn back. In an airplane, you are thrown to an absolute death and witnesses watch your body fall. In the death house, you are strapped to a gurney and witnesses watch state officials inject you with sodium pentothal. In both cases, death is sudden and final.

To me they are the same. I will feel the same powerful emotions and chaotic anxiety either way. But the public would never describe my death by falling from an aircraft as "simply falling asleep." They would be outraged. Politicians would rush to give speeches about giving prisoners a "choice," and the law would be changed.

The public would cry out, not because the prisoner died an agonizing and painful death but because most people feel that the anxiety of being tossed from an aircraft without a parachute would be too terrible for an inmate to bear, and the spectacle of death would be too terrible for observers to bear. In this case, the public would be forced to understand the emotions an inmate feels before execution; when lethal injection is used, all such emotions are hidden behind a veil that is not drawn aside until the moment before death.

This airplane analogy is as close as I can come to illustrating the fallacy of the humane execution. There is much more to death by injection than just falling asleep, beginning with the long wait on death row (where execution is a constant presence), the terror of being taken to the death house, the helpless panic of being strapped to a table, and finally the sense of utter loss as the curtain is opened. All of the fear and anxiety of falling from an aircraft is present when the injection begins. Both are horrible by any measure. And neither is anything like falling asleep.

Fighting for Life

Blake R. Pirtle

Blake R. Pirtle was sentenced to death in 1993 for murdering two restaurant employees during a robbery. While he never denied his guilt, he claimed that several of his civil rights were violated during his trial. He filed an appeal that resulted in his sentence being changed to life without parole.

In the following article Pirtle discusses his experience in Washington State's supermax control unit. He describes how he struggled to survive by reaching out to others with a spirit of humility. By taking full responsibility for his actions, he says, he has learned to love himself. He shares his belief that the death penalty is unjust because by the time a death sentence is carried out the convicted person has usually gone through many personality changes and is, in fact, not the same individual who was originally sentenced. Pirtle insists that he is not the same man and wants to use his second chance at life to be a positive influence for others.

Life After Death

I can very clearly still remember the day that a jury of my so-called peers told me that they thought I should die for my crimes. I sat there in disbelief, not feeling anything or showing any type of emotion at all. All I could think was that I don't blame them; it's not their fault. The 13 of us had just sat through a meaningless trial where I was painted as the worst person that you could imagine. We sat through a trial full of lies and deceit. As a matter of fact, the only truth that took place during the whole trial was my defense and testimony. So I could not sit there and hold any grudge against the 12 jurors that had just been convinced to murder me in the name of justice.

Blake R. Pirtle, "Life After Death," *Cell Door Magazine,* vol 3, November 2001. Reproduced by permission.

In fact, I felt bad for them. I had killed myself and was still trying to come to grips with the terrible choices I had made. And here were 12 honest, hard working citizens that had just decided to kill me and they had been convinced to do it through lies and deceit. The only difference at that point between them and myself was that I did what I did and it was against the law. They were going to be able to hide behind the mask of so-called justice. I just hoped that they would be able to sleep better at night than I did. I never once denied my guilt. So my trial had no purpose at all, except to ensure that I received the death penalty.

For 6 long weeks I had to sit there and listen to the lies and deceit, wondering the whole time if maybe it may all be true. Did I just not see it? It was, in fact, the most helpless that I have ever felt in my whole life. Who were people going to believe? The police, detectives, jailhouse snitches, and prosecutors? Or a man that had killed two people in the course of a robbery? Well, you figure it out. I couldn't challenge the lies and deceit because I had no credibility. Even though from the beginning of it all I had stood up and accepted responsibility, I left the courthouse that day on my way to death row, feeling ashamed, broken, and beat down. Little did I know that by not challenging the lies and deceit at that time 8 years later it was going to rescue me from hell!

Finding the Courage to Live

The strange thing about being told that you are a monster and should die for your crimes and sins against man is that if you hear it enough and really listen to it, you start to believe it and agree. And starting my life on death row here at Walla Walla [location of Washington State Penitentiary] only increased the self-pity 100 fold. I entered my life here on death row, pretty well beaten even though I was saying all the right things. I will fight this until the end, the death penalty is unjust, and doesn't apply to me. The Death Penalty doesn't deter violent crime. It is only a sentence of revenge.

Everything I felt and said was soon going to be tested to the limit. My introduction to life in prison was being placed right into a super max control unit. A unit set up and designed by the department of corrections to break down troublemakers and get them to change their aggressive behavior. It is a very effective unit too. But more times than not, it doesn't rehabilitate a problem inmate; it drives most inmates over the edge and creates many more problems.

So this was my new world. Why was I being housed in a punishment unit? My sentence of course. So I entered IMU, already feeling broken and on edge. After being thrust into this incredibly insane environment, I was expected to have the strength and desire to fight for my life? Now that was hard. Already I had been told so often that I was a monster that I was starting to believe it. Now I was going to be treated like an animal for the next 8 years with only a few short breaks in between.

The best way to describe a super max unit to anyone that has never experienced one is to ask you to go to the dog pound and visit the dangerous dog section for a while. I was placed in a very small cell 23 hours a day, the light was never turned off, and I was fed through a small slot in the solid steel door. I got one hour in the exercise yard a day and a 10-minute shower. I did not leave my cell without being strip-searched first, handcuffed, placed on a dog leash with a two-guard escort. If I needed to shave I stood naked in the shower while a guard stood right there and watched me shave. This is the environment that I had to find the strength, desire, and courage to live and fight for my life.

Coming to Death Row

I was 22 years old when I murdered 2 people in the course of a robbery. I was 24 years old when I was told I should die for my crimes. I entered my life on death row here at Walla Walla a very narrow minded, uneducated, emotionally distressed kid. I had very little support because all of the people that I considered friends no longer found me worthy of any type of companionship. The one thing that I had going for me that many people in my position do not have was that I had a very large family. Most of them were there to support me in my fight for life. No, they did not condone what I had done. No one should! But their love for me never died and that is something that I will always be very thankful for. The other thing I carried with me into this life of death row that truly consumed me at times was a huge amount of guilt and remorse for what I had done. I knew within a week of my arrival on death row that I had better find a comfort zone—some way to balance the guilt that I suffered. If I could not do that, then my fight for life would be unsuccessful, that's for sure.

After and during a trial of this nature, you are pounded and beat down with everything that was bad in your life and all the bad things that you did. You start to buy into the thoughts and ideas because things in your life were not perfect—in some cases, downright insane. You begin to believe that you yourself had no chance at being good and something of this nature was bound to happen. And none of it is really your fault. You start to feel and believe that it was your destiny so to speak to be evil and bad. I also carried a lot of that within myself. It took me years to be able to focus on anything besides the bad things.

But I started to adjust to my life on death row. Soon the confined space of my cell no longer bothered me. I enjoyed the solitude. I do, in fact, credit the super max unit for the mindset and strength I have today. I could deal with the cell, the light staying on 24 hours; I got used to it. The noise was another matter; it was enough to drive you insane. I learned to make and wear earplugs so I could think, and sleep. I even got used to the strip searches and showing my asshole to the guards. Once I learned that they did not enjoy looking at it as much as I hated showing it to them, I started to have some fun with it. I would get as close to the door as I could, spread my butt cheeks as far as I could and hold the pose for an extra minute or so at least until they said okay that's good.

Becoming Proactive

I understood right away that I could not fight this fight alone. My family was great, but they could only do so much. So I started to contact every death penalty support group that I could. I started to place ads everywhere that I could think of. Soon the letters started to pour in from all over the world. Strangers from everywhere wrote to me to extend their hand of friendship and help me fight this fight. The smartest choice I every made in my life was to not approach any of these friendships as a hustle or a game. Not to go into it for self-gain or material items. To be completely honest with anyone that took the time to write to me, no matter how hard or painful it was. Because of that simple choice, I have been able to develop and enjoy some of the most rewarding, loving, and unconditional friendships that I have ever experienced. That has been completely priceless, and the very thing that has kept me going for these last 8 years.

My next step was get involved with my appeals. I knew nothing about the appeal process, the law or the courts. Even though I had been in quite a bit of trouble in my past, it was all alien to me. I had never come close to going to prison and never went to trial. I always took the best deal and pled guilty to my crimes. Got my slap on the hand from the system and moved on. So this whole appeal process was new to me.

I was soon to learn that appeals can be a complete nightmare. Thankfully, I have and had some very great attorneys throughout it all. I hated every step of this damn appeal process. First, I learned that I had made a terrible mistake—admitting my guilt. So many times I had to read from judges and courts, "Well there is no doubt to his guilt" and I was like no shit, I've admitted it from the start. But because I did, do I have to die for my crimes? It sure looked that way for quite some time. All I can say now is, if facing the death penalty, never admit your guilt no matter if you feel it's the right thing to do or not. It will only be used against you!

Learning to Love Myself

The next step and by far the hardest one that I needed to accomplish to succeed in my fight for life was this. I had to learn to love myself again! No, not forgive myself because I don't think I could ever truly forgive myself for what I did. But to love myself! I have never really hated anything or anyone in my whole life, but after I did what I did and after going through my trial I flat out hated myself. I hated the way I lived my life and the choices I made. I hated that I had murdered two very innocent people that had every right to live. I hated that, through my actions, I had destroyed my own life along with many others. I hated to even look at myself in the mirror. Thankfully the cells in IMU have no mirrors so that is something that I didn't have to do often. Because of the solitude of the super max unit, I was able to look deep within myself. What I soon discovered was that the guilt I suffered was in fact a good thing. I couldn't deny it, run from it or act like what I did did not trouble me. What I had to do was embrace it and not let it consume me. It would forever be a part of my life; I just couldn't let it control my life. I also was able to look deep within myself and love myself. I had to see more than just the bad. People are not born bad, they choose to be bad and they choose to do bad things. I realized that not everything about myself was in fact bad, not everything about my life or childhood was bad. It would only remain bad if I chose to only see the bad.

I realized that I had a strong desire to change, to be good and do good things with my life. Deep down inside of me I had a good heart and felt like I was a good person. But now how do I show others this? How do I try to do good and give something, no matter how small, back? I do believe that I have made great strides in this area, and it wasn't easy. I also learned that I was a very stubborn man. I was very set in a lot of my dysfunctional ways. This is still and always will be a work in progress. I learned that it's a whole lot harder to be good and make good, smart choices in your life than to be bad and selfish. But after about 2 years I was able to start to love myself again and become a completely different person than I was on that day in 1993 when a jury sentenced me to death. No, I do not give myself all the credit. I would have never grown into the person I am today without the guidance, love, and support from the hundreds of strangers that blessed my life. But I do give credit to myself for the complete honesty and openness with which I approached them. Without that everything would have remained meaningless and I would not have changed one bit.

The Appeals Roller Coaster

There is no way that I could possibly explain the process of a death penalty appeal to you all or what life on death row is like. It is one huge roller-coaster ride of emotions and a total mind f---. The reason so many people give up their appeals and let the government kill them is not out of guilt for their crimes or remorse, but because emotionally they just cannot take it anymore. I reached that point many of times myself. I would sit in this cell and ask myself, "What the hell am I even fighting for? What's the point of it all? I have an easy way out, a way to stop all my pain and misery."

In my past I always took the easy way out. I always gave up when things got too hard to deal with. Whether it was through drug abuse, or just walking away from my responsibilities. I bailed out, took the chickenshit way out. Well not this time! Even if it was to be spent forever in prison, I would fight for life to the very bitter end. Win or lose at least I would be able to say that for once I fought for something I felt passionate about. For 8 long years I dealt with the appeal process. Many times, it completely drained me. At times things would look so good, my issues seemed so strong. At others times, I would feel like I had no chance of winning at all. Up and down I rode this bronco, always trying to stay positive and never letting my fears show. Those of you who have written to me over the years have seen this and lived it with me. Even though I knew I didn't have to, I've tried so hard to keep my emotional duress out of my letters and phone calls to you. Well, I am happy to report to all of you readers that the ride from hell is just about over for me and that this is a success story. On June 28, 2001 a Federal Judge out of Spokane, Washington, overturned my sentence of death. I still write to you from death row waiting to be moved, but as I write my sentence is no longer death, but stands at life without parole.

You Are Killing a Different Person

I know I titled this column Life After Death. Some of you may not comprehend the depth of that. For 8 years now no matter how good things looked or how positive I was about my future, I have truly felt like I was just waiting around to die. Time had no meaning for me whatsoever because I knew that, if it ran its course, I was going to be hung by my government. So I truly feel as if I have been given a whole new life and a new destiny to fulfill in this life. The death penalty and the appeal process are to me by far the cruelest thing you can put a human being through. Now I know that might sound very strange coming from a self-admitted murderer of two people. But look at it through my eyes. Yes, I murdered two people. But it happened in a split second—an irrational choice made in a moment of time. If they knew at all that they were in fact going to die, it was very, very briefly. I on the other hand have been forced to think about my own death for over

8 years now. And think about it I did, every single day—the countless sleepless nights walking the gallows stairs. I can still remember very clearly when I lost my first appeal and had to go to court to have an execution date set. Even though I knew it would never happen and I would have a stay within hours, I can still remember walking out of that courtroom, seeing the complete fear in my baby sister's eyes. Then on the drive back to Walla Walla wondering, "Doesn't anyone else find it morbid that a date, time and hour was just set to kill me?"

Capital punishment is one of the most shameful acts that the United States is guilty of. I would not wish the process or life on my worst enemies and that is the truth! You see, when we kill someone through the process of capital punishment, 90% of the time we are not killing the same person that committed the horrible act that placed them on death row. You are in fact killing a completely different person! You have given them 10, 15, or 20 years to grow and change into someone else. I am a perfect example of that. If my execution had ever been carried out, they would not have killed the drug addicted kid that murdered two people. They would be killing a man that had changed in so many ways that most people from my past would not even believe that I was the same person.

I have known now for almost 2 years that I was going to win my appeal. The way things developed and the way the law supported my issues, left me with no doubt that I was going to win. But for me to sit here and tell you that it washed away all my doubts and fears would be for me to sit here and lie to you. No matter how good things look or appear nothing is certain when you're dealing with the death penalty. No one can guess or predict how a judge or court is going to rule in your case. To do so is flat out asinine! But 2 years of looking at my issues and the law that supported me told me I was going to win. But in the last year I became completely sure that I would win. Call it faith, call it whatever you please. But this is what convinced me. As I have told you I made great strides in becoming a good person, so that's part of it. But in the last year I have been blessed with a love that I thought I would never be capable of experiencing again. My life was blessed with a couple of childhood friends from my past that mean the world to me. And my son Devon who was born while I was waiting to go to trial has now become a huge part of my life after 8 1/2 years. So I knew deep in my heart that there was no way that God, or whoever you like, would bring these elements into my life, would bless me in so many ways, if it wasn't in fact my destiny to be around for a very long time to rekindle and enjoy the beauty of it all.

I Will Become a Better Man

My story and appeal is a success for a bigger reason than just delivering me from the insane sentence of death. It is a success because through my case we were able to set and establish some great case law that is going to help many more condemned people in their appeals. This fight wasn't about innocence like so many are. It was about justice and your constitutional rights. Rights that are guaranteed to every American and yet are violated so often by the government and police, and ignored by the courts. The greatest pleasure I get out of all of this is knowing that, by fighting and never giving up, I may in fact be helping to deliver many others from the evil sentence of death!

From the very start of all of this I have tried my very best to become a better person in life. I have made great strides in doing just this with very limited resources available to me. Now since my life and my whole world are about to change, so many more things will be available to me to continue in my growth process. I will continue to strive to do good and look forward to it very much. Hopefully soon I will be able to write a column about all the changes in my life and how I am applying them in a positive way. Never once throughout all of this have I allowed myself to feel self-pity or sorry for myself. I made the choices in life and did the things that landed me where I am. No, it was not the fault of the drugs or a violent, abusive childhood. Yes, they may have guided me on the paths that I chose to take in my life. That is the key statement. The choices I made! I hold myself completely responsible for all the things that I did in life. I do carry a heavy burden of guilt and remorse for the lives that I have turned upside down and destroyed. I will always carry that burden. Not too many people could walk in my shoes, or endure the shame I do. But I will not let that stop me from continuing to grow and become a better man.

Now I know that, to most everyone, a life without the possibility of release or parole is not something that would be seen as a good thing. In a lot of ways, I don't either. But it beats the hell out of death. The difference is that I will be alive. I know I can create a life for myself even from behind these steel bars and walls. I also feel that I will accomplish great things that will make many proud to know me and be a part of my life. I also, even though it's hard to admit, feel that I have no right, considering what I did, to expect to ever have a life outside of prison.

America's Death Penalty System Is Broken

Ray Krone with Alan M. Simpson

Ray Krone was a postal carrier when he was arrested in 1991 for the murder of Kim Ancona, a local bartender who worked in a Phoenix lounge where Krone played darts. In 1992 he was convicted and sentenced to death. In 2002 DNA evidence linked another man to the crime, and Krone was released from prison after serving ten years for a crime he did not commit.

In the following selection Krone describes the details of his false imprisonment and his desire to make sure that others will not have to suffer a similar fate. Krone now speaks publicly in favor of criminal justice reform, the abolishment of the death penalty, and the accountability of law enforcement agencies. After his 2002 release Maricopa County, Arizona, awarded Krone a $1.4 million settlement for his suffering and loss.

America's Death-Penalty System Is Broken

I'm not a Pulitzer Prize-winning columnist. Or a politician. Or the head of any organization. I'm simply an average American. An average American who sat on Death Row.

My name is Ray Krone. I grew up in York, Pa., with a loving family and many friends. I played Little League baseball, went hiking with the Cub Scouts and Boy Scouts, attended Sunday school and sang in the church choir. I graduated in the top 10 percent of my high school class and did well on my college entrance exams. I decided to enlist in the Air Force, where I proudly attained the rank of sergeant. I served my country for seven years and was honorably discharged. My last

This death row inmate gets exercise in an exercise pen at San Quentin's death row in California. © Clay Mclachlan/Reuters/CORBIS

assignment in the Air Force was in Arizona. I decided to stay there, and joined the U.S. Postal Service.

I had a normal, good life. Nothing spectacular. Then, in an instant, my life was turned upside down. I was arrested for the stabbing murder of a local female bartender. At the time, and quite frankly, throughout the whole legal process, I truly felt I would be OK. After all, I was innocent. I reassured my family and friends I would be fine without a private attorney. How could the system fail an innocent man? I was deeply mistaken.

It was a bar I frequented, and I did know the bartender. Thanks to some bad forensic science, bite marks on the body were mistakenly said to have been made by my teeth.

I spent 10 years behind bars, including two years on Death Row for a horrible crime I did not commit. It's difficult to describe what it is like to serve time on Death Row knowing you are innocent. All you know is that what seems like an awful nightmare is now reality, a reality beyond comprehension.

The DNA Proved My Innocence

I still find it hard to believe that only a few weeks ago I was sitting in my Arizona jail cell and today I am a free man. I owe my freedom to the extraordinary efforts of my family, friends and volunteer lawyers who fought tirelessly for me to obtain the DNA evidence from my case. The DNA proved my innocence—and a match has now been been made with the DNA of another man.

What happened to me, unfortunately, has happened to many others. True, I have recently received notoriety—if it can be called that—for being the 100th American exonerated, but the fact is that being 100 or 99 or 98 doesn't really matter. What matters is that our death-penalty system is broken. What happened to me can happen to anyone. And it doesn't have to be that way.

I've learned a lot in the last few weeks of freedom. And one thing I've learned is that there are steps our nation can take to improve our death-penalty system. One important step would be for Congress to pass the Innocence Protection Act. This act would ensure that people who face the death penalty have greater access to the DNA from their cases. And it would also help states provide competent legal counsel in capital punishment cases.

Curiously enough, I still believe in our system of justice. But like any system, it can be improved. I'm not asking members of Congress to change their views on the death penalty. I have to believe, however, that even those who support the death penalty do not support putting innocent people to their death—and leaving the guilty to roam free.

Ten years ago, I was an average Joe who liked delivering the mail. Today, I'm still an American with average dreams, but I've had a lot more time to think about things.

I can't afford to look back at what my life would have been like if I had obtained access to the DNA from my case years ago or if I had listened to my mother and hired a private attorney. For me, there is no sense in dwelling on what might have been. The time has come to look at what can be. And helping to make sure that what happened to me is less likely to happen to someone else is a much better use of my precious time.

Views of Participants in the Death Penalty

Ministering to Inmates Facing Execution

Carroll Pickett, interview by PBS

The Reverend Carroll Pickett was a death house chaplain in Huntsville, Texas, for sixteen years. He helped ninety-five men confront the reality of their imminent deaths before he retired from the Department of Criminal Justice in 1995.

In the following excerpt from an interview conducted by the Public Broadcasting Service, Pickett discusses the rituals that take place during the last few hours before a prisoner's execution. While there are state-mandated steps that must be followed, every man is different when it comes to choosing how he will spend his final hours. Some are silent, some sleep, but most just want an ear to hear the things that have burdened them for so long. Pickett contends that the years of waiting are the most inhumane part of the death penalty process. Most men sit on death row in a five-foot-by-nine-foot cell for years before reaching the death house.

Pickett says he never wanted to stay in the death house for so long. Initially intending to serve as death chaplain for one year, Pickett remained because, he said, "I've always felt like the hardest thing to do would be to have to die alone."

Pickett wrote The Team Concept of Execution, *which is the protocol followed by most states currently administering death by lethal injection. Now an abolitionist, Pickett has published* Within These Walls: Memoirs of a Death House Chaplain.

Death Chaplain

PBS: What are the most frequently asked questions in those last hours?

Carroll Pickett, "The Execution," Frontline, PBS/WBGH February 9, 1999. Copyright © 1999 by WGBH Media Library. Reproduced by permission.

Carroll Pickett: 'Am I going to see the victim's family?' And I was always able to say, No. They are not permitted to be here.

Was that a relief or a disappointment?

That was a great relief for the men. In my opinion, that was one of the biggest fears that they had. They just didn't want to see the [victim's] family.

They may begin to allow the families of victims in now. Would you be opposed to that?

From listening to the men that I've been with, for their sake it's going to be a problem. If I just look at it strictly from their viewpoint. If they see their five family over here and the other five over here, I think it would make a lot of difference, and it's going to take a lot of preparation to talk to the man. Because one of the things that we do during this process is explaining everything. I ask him what his final statement is going to be. Not that I want to word his statement for him. Not that I want to teach him what to say or tell him what to say, but in order to know in advance if he knows what he is going to say so we won't stop his message.

Lots of times they just want me to help word it. What they want to get across is a message and they're going to have two or three minutes. They know they can't read it. Some of them asked me, Would you read it for me? No. I can't do that. Some of them ask me, you know, if I stumble will you go ahead and since you know what I'm going to say will you finish it for me? I couldn't do that because those would not be his last words. They'd be my last words. That's one of the things that we prepare. We do discuss his final statement and they will tell me what it is. And most the time they stick with it real close.

Rituals Before Death

Then midnight comes. What happens? Or now, it's been changed to 6:00 in the evening.

Some of them want to watch a clock. Most of them don't want to watch a clock. They want me to tell them what time it is, and if they don't want to know, then I don't tell them. And it seemed to work easier because then they don't become clock-watchers. They write their letters and so forth. Come 12:00, I'll tell them, 'it is 12:00.' And when the warden steps through I'll say, 'it is time to go.' I step back, the doors are unlocked, the two officers who have been there, along with three more who are coming in, serve as sort of an escort. And there is three on one side and two on the other. And I walk into the execution chamber. He follows me. I've already explained to him where to go and how to sit, which direction, and where to place his feet and then the officers help out quite a bit.

There is something of a ceremony to it all, isn't there?

I think there is a ritual. There are certain things that the law prescribes. There are certain things that have to be done to make it proper and there are all those general things that change like who we get to visit him and who we get to talk to. Also, each one is different. Some of them have been willing to talk, talk, talk and some of them just want to remain totally silent. Some of them want to talk about different things, you know, from family to history. Some of them want to spend a lot of time disputing the news accounts, what's in the paper. Sometimes when we used to have a radio down there it was on. But every one of them is different. Everyone has certain elements that nobody else has done.

Honesty in the Last Moments

Do you think there have been some you have watched die who were strictly innocent?

I never felt that. The last two hours of every one of them they are ... I would say [are] more than honest. And they want to talk about things that a lot of people don't know and a lot of people are going to never know, because I'm not going to tell ... they just want to talk about things that may have been sitting there on their hearts and their spirits and their souls for a long, long time.

Confessions?

Many.

Of the crimes and other things.

Yes.

And do they seem to feel better after doing this?

Yes. I have seen some of them who, after a confession—I'm going to use your term confession; I just call it being reality at the last minute—they would lie down and go to sleep at 11:30. Just take a brief nap. It's just like they got some weight that they've been carrying around. They can just lie down on that ... in Cell 1 and just take a nap. There are two or three of them I have had to wake up at five minutes to 12.

They take a nap with a half hour to live?

Very few of them but there has been some.

Are there some who are inconsolable for whom you've not been able to offer any help?

There have been a couple. One of them just did not talk to anybody. Nobody. There have been a couple of them who came in and said they didn't want to talk, but after a couple hours I will just tell them, Okay, if that's your choice, I will be available. I will not leave the unit, or I can go down to Cell 7 and be out of the way. But basically . . . of the 95 that I have been with all the way, there has been only one who refused to talk at all.

It's Important to Remain Neutral

Do you get to like some enough that it really hurts you to see him die?

Some of the men have changed from what they used to be. Those who came in particularly as 17- or 18-year-olds and stay a long, long time. You know you can change. Everybody changes at 16 years or 14 years or 8 years. Some of them change tremendously in two years. There are some of them that I have really found to be very interesting, friendly, and this is very hypothetical, yet sometimes I felt like if we could have been friends had they been in another situation at another time.

Which is one of the main arguments against the death penalty—that you are killing a different person than the one who committed the murders. When I talked to you, you weren't able or willing to say how you feel about the death penalty because you work for the system. Can you now?

I don't think that I can. Maybe it's because I don't really know. I can sit back now and look at 13 years of being in there, almost 16 in the chaplaincy, and 13 years of doing it being the chaplain to the death house, not death row. And as I look at the world, I can see that this process is not cutting down on what's going on out in the free world. That is one of the arguments if it's a deterrent to crime in the world. I mean it's just a fact. Anybody can tell you that. It's not working. Getting it may be to that person. I've preferred to just leave that alone. That's a question that I couldn't answer then and I can't answer it now. Then . . . if I said I was opposed to it, they'd fire me. You couldn't work for the system . . . if I said I was in favor of it, then some of the inmates wouldn't want to talk.

You purposely didn't get to know these men until the last few hours. Is that correct?

That's right. That was a decision made by director Mr. Stell back in the early '80s, and he set up the procedure that he wanted a chaplain to deal with them out there . . . and to keep it separate. I didn't like the term death chaplain but that's the way he put it.

Over the last years, I've talked to more than 30 states. They've come here with us or learned or taught, and I've been to some other states. And I recommend that . . . where a man is a chaplain to an individual for four, five, six years. They get involved with his family and they get over his life and it's difficult for them. I know in some states they have not been able to walk the last mile.

The minister hasn't?

Right. And I have talked to the chaplain and I told the warden about that, and I really think that Mr. Stell was right. They know that we start fresh in here. I don't go back and read these guys' transcripts. Whatever they want to tell me, you know, whereas the fellow out there will know his whole life history. They'll know whether he had been a good convict or bad convict. Whether he's attended church or mass or the Islamic services. I can start clean, and I think that's the best way.

Willard Trulove, who was sentenced to death for a 1949 murder, prays in his cell before being sent to the electric chair. © Bettmann/CORBIS

I Didn't Set Out to Do Executions

I'm trying to get a sense of the kind of struggle this may have been for you, either with each execution or continually. Are those fair words to use for the kind of career you had for 16 years?

47

The struggle goes on. There were many times I did not go to sleep. There were many times when I felt like, not that we did anything wrong, but maybe we could have done something better, particularly, you know, one young kid in his 20s. You know that was difficult because I had kids that were older than 20. And that's been several years ago, but that was something that it took several, several days to even come to grips with what had taken place. And nothing bad took place. It's just that I can see the look on his face, and this event took place eight years ago. There . . . with each one of them I can go back and pick out a name and there's something unique about it.

. . . I was speaking to a group at a high school in Marion, Ohio, earlier this year. And one of the young kids asked the question, 'When are you going to snap?' And I have had that in my mind for a long time. I think it's always going to be there.

Have you come close?

There have been times when I've almost decided I didn't want to do it anymore.

You set out to do it for one year and you did it for 16 years. What kept you going?

I didn't set out to do executions. I set out to do a chaplaincy. At the time, it was never in my job description. I think the one thing that kept me going was not only my faith but this to me was a great important part of ministry. I made a commitment to a man in my first church. A man by the name of Dan Miller, who had no family, down in a little town of Senton, Texas, and he asked me, Would you stay with me while I die? He was dying of cancer, and I made a promise to him that if it's within my power to help you when you die, I'll be there. I was 23 at the time. Just barely out of seminary.

And I kept that promise, or tried to in all of my three pastorates that I've had since him. Then also there in prison. . . . It was the same way. So it is part of my ministry to be with the person who dies who can't have family there. I've always felt that the hardest thing to do would be have to die alone. My premise over all the years is not that a man should die alone. If I can be with him for six hours, eight hours, 12 hours, 24 hours, and help him die not alone then that's what kept me going.

Weren't there times some evenings—seeing this man scared out of his wits, perhaps talking to members of his family who are grief stricken—when you want to say, 'Let him live. Let's not go through with it.'

I could never say that. The law was in control. The law of the state of Texas, and that was the thing that was told us at the very beginning. This is going to happen whether you are here or not, and I would prefer to stay with him and try to help him and listen to him. And if he needed a Dr. Pepper, get him a Dr. Pepper. If he needed a particular song, I'd find him that song. If he wanted to sing, we'd sing, and I don't sing well. I knew I never had the power to stop it.

The Punishment Is in Waiting

Can you think of anything that people miss on this issue of capital punishment?

It's been hashed and rehashed and spoken and studied so much. Today the biggest problem about the whole procedure is the length of time they must wait, between the time they get convicted and the time they carry it out. That to me will always be a problem. They want you to have to stay years and years and years . . . that's not living. That's really not living.

That's what some of them say. That the punishment is not the execution, but the waiting.

Oh, so many of them! When they get here, they're relieved. It's like getting it over with. You've been living for a decade and a half knowing that you can't go home. You've got a 5 x 9. And for people of faith who believe in an afterlife, this is a freedom. It's the only freedom these people are going to get. It just takes so long and to me ... that's the punishment part. Because everybody's going to die one way or another. But to have to live your last 15 years in a 5 x 9, that's worse, and a lot harder in my opinion.

A State Prosecutor's View of the Death Penalty

John Connelly, interview by Paul Bass

The following selection is excerpted from an interview of Connecticut state's attorney John Connelly, conducted by Paul Bass, a reporter for the Hartford Advocate *newspaper. Connelly, who has been nicknamed the "Death Penalty King," unapologetically discusses his commitment to pursuing the death penalty where it falls within the parameters of the law. Connelly has been in the state's attorney's office since 1980, and five of the seven of the state's death row inmates owe their convictions to Connelly's efforts. While interviewer Paul Bass repeatedly questions the ethical implications of sending someone to his or her death, Connelly insists that seeking capital convictions is simply his job and that he has no personal agenda in pursuing the death penalty.*

While Connelly has always supported the death penalty, he has also received the local NAACP's "Humanitarian Award" for "courage in applying justice equally in all cases" and "his long-standing commitment to mankind in every aspect of his life."

Hartford Advocate: How does it feel being known as the death penalty king?

John Connelly: I just hope you're known as the person who does the job as it's supposed to be done. Who's not afraid. Who's not lazy. Who puts the time into these cases. It would be easier to give them 40 years for pleading guilty. Would you be doing your job then?

You have to make the decision of whether to go for the death penalty. That's up to the prosecutor.

Paul Bass, "Inside the Mind of the Prosecutor Who put Away Five of Connecticut's Seven Death-Row Inmates,," interview with John Connelly, *Hartford Advocate*, December 13, 2001. Copyright © 2001 by New Mass Media, Inc. All rights reserved. Reproduced by permission.

What happens [is]: Somebody's charged. Then we look at the case. . . . We sit down with the leading [police] officer involved. There's an assistant state's attorney here, Maureen Keegan, who's done all these cases with me. We sit down with the inspector from the [prosecutor's] office who worked on the case. [We ask:] Is there any question in our minds that the person did the crime? Are there aggravating factors here? Are there any mitigating factors?

Part of this is discretion. . . .

Now, there are eight types of murders that qualify as capital felonies: Murder of a police officer. Murder of two or more people in the course of a single transaction. Murder of someone under 16. Murder in the course of a kidnapping. Murder in the course of a sexual assault. . . . So if this case qualifies as a capital felony, we'll take it to the judge and present evidence for finding probable cause. If the judge finds probable cause, that doesn't mean the death penalty's going to follow, know what I'm saying?

But you personally decide whether to seek the death penalty?

. . . if we have enough to go for the capital felony.

Two cases where the court found probable cause, before we went to trial, we reviewed the case and decided that we could not go forward even with the capital felony charge. So I guess we did exercise discretion. In one of those cases [a woman] gave birth to a baby unbeknownst to anyone in the house, in her bedroom, and the baby ultimately died shortly thereafter. So that's a capital felony because she was under 16. We got probable cause for capital felony. Just after giving birth there was a question whether we could prove the baby was born live. We allowed her to plead guilty to manslaughter. She got 20 years.

Another case was a drug case. Up until last year [2000] if you sold drugs to someone for profit, and he died as a result of that, that was a capital felony. We always felt uncomfortable with that. We got the probable cause finding for the capital felony. But as we proceeded through, I felt uncomfortable. I didn't feel the Supreme Court would ultimately uphold that statute. And in fact it was ultimately [changed by the legislature].

It's Just Part of My Job

You say you were "uncomfortable." Were you uncomfortable with the idea of a person dying because of this? Or were you uncomfortable with the idea that you wouldn't succeed?

I was uncomfortable because, yeah, we just didn't think the statute was proper.

"Proper" in terms of it not passing muster with the Supreme Court? If it could pass muster with the Supreme Court, would you want to prosecute it?

I think we would have.

The case we're doing now is [Robert] Courchesne. He stabbed to death a woman who was nine months pregnant. There was a Caesarean. The baby [died].

After all these years, do you get used to talking about cases where someone squished a baby's head?

Yeah, you do.

Is that an adjustment? Psychologically, how do you deal with it?

It's a job, you know what I'm saying? As a reporter, as a photographer, you cover gruesome scenes. It's just part of your job. . . .

My Job Is to Enforce the Law

My guess is if [some other Connecticut prosecutors] sat in your chair, there wouldn't be as many people on death row.

Our job is to enforce the law. Whether or not we like the law. I don't think people should wear seat belts.

Really?

I'm just saying. It's a hypothetical. Let's say I felt the government didn't have the right to tell people they have to wear seat belts. Does that mean I don't enforce the seat belt law?

If there were a capital litigation unit devoted purely to seat belt cases, and they were filing reams of motions, they were going to make you sweat and work on nothing else but seat belt cases, would you still fight it?

Sure.

There's still discretion. You decide how much you're going to go to the mat for different cases.

You can abuse your discretion both ways. You can abuse your discretion by bringing cases that don't fall within the law, right? And you can abuse your discretion by *not* bringing cases that fall within the law.

So you feel if you hadn't tried these cases [as death penalty cases], you'd be abusing your discretion?

Right.

But you didn't bring those [capital] cases with the drugs, because you didn't feel that law passed muster. So theoretically you could have done that with some of these other cases.

If you look at these five cases, if you look at the seven people on [Connecticut's] death row, the victims are all either women or children, except [with] Richard Reynolds, who killed a police officer.

So what do you take from that?

The murders they committed were horrendous murders. They were committed against little kids and women. These are people who society should be protecting, right? All these guys are bullies. Who do they pick on? Even Reynolds. Reynolds was a drug dealer before he shot [Walter] Williams. He bumped into him to make sure he didn't have a bulletproof vest on. He found he had a bulletproof vest on. He put a gun to Williams' head and shot him.

Race "Nonsense"

People criticize the death penalty on racial grounds. . . .

You know, opponents of the death penalty, they used to say, look at the race of the perpetrator. . . . Now they argue, "Look at the race of the victims." Which is nonsense.

Why is that nonsense?

What does that have anything to do with it?

Because they're saying that juries and judges are more outraged if the victims were white.

That's nonsense. That's nonsense. It is. Who's ever said that, it's nonsense. I have not seen that. Juries do not base their decisions on the race of the victim.

Blacks get killed in black-on-black crime. Why do you think to date none [of those killers] are on death row?

Whether or not they qualify. Not all murders are susceptible to the death penalty. You have to come in on one of those eight categories.

In New Haven, an 8-month-old girl was murdered [by a drug dealer in 1993] . . .

You have to ask [New Haven State's Attorney] Mike Dearington about that. In the Kenya Best case, there was a black woman who beat to death her black child. We brought that case. The three-judge panel found it to be manslaughter. The other case was Alfredo Marty. The baby was mixed-race. Those are cases where we brought as capital felony cases, they were tried as capital felony cases. . . .

So that might be evidence for what they're saying.

That's three judges. Then you have to question three judges. Six judges altogether, right?

They are questioning.

They question everything. They would not agree with the death penalty in any case. They will not give you a scenario where the death penalty is appropriate. How can you argue with that? By showing them statistics, by showing them anything, you're not going to be able to convert them.

No Second Thoughts

A lot of people have changed their minds about the death penalty. You must have read about Illinois Gov. George Ryan [a pro–death penalty Republican who ordered a moratorium on executions after revelations about death row inmates actually being innocent]. Pat Robertson. Does this impact you at all? Do you think there's a change in public opinion?

Not the people I talk to.

What I worry about, my concern, are the cases that we prosecute. I don't know about [Illinois]. If someone is on death row and clearly is not guilty, you can't have a graver injustice, can you?

So you don't believe there's any kind of reconsideration going on in this country?

How about all the people on death row who are indeed guilty? Who committed horrendous crimes? You don't hear about those people. You hear about the one or two who had a lawyer who was sleeping. Those are terrible cases. They should be corrected. I think it's disingenuous to use those examples as the way the system works in general.

I think the system we have is a good system. The judges I've dealt with are concerned with defendants' rights, especially in capital cases. The people of the state of Connecticut are concerned about it. We have a very good unit that defends these cases. They put two lawyers on every case.

Other industrialized nations do not have the death penalty.

I've read a study which said that the people of Sweden, I think by 65 percent, would want the death penalty.

So why do you think they don't have it?

I think it's the type of governments they have [in Europe]....

They're elected governments.

Yeah, but they're not republican, like we are. They are parliamentary types. They have minority parties.

We also have representative government. We protect against a majority that goes against our basic principles.

The United States isn't like any other country. The diversity of population. Look at the amount of crime we get. The amount of civil liberties we have.

We have more crimes . . .

Because we have more liberties, see what I'm saying? So when you compare the United States to other countries, you're not really comparing apples to apples.

So do you think the price of our liberty is the death penalty?

Going back to the seat belt analogy, I can't enforce or not enforce what I think is good or bad. Our legislature made the decision. In our system of government, the legislature represents the majority of people. They said the death penalty is appropriate punishment for certain crimes.

Why Do We Need the Death Penalty?

Do you think the death penalty deters people from committing crimes?

Well, one of the crimes that the death penalty applies to is murder of a corrections officer. You've got to ask yourself: How many corrections officers in Connecticut have been murdered? The answer is zero. So you can argue that it deters the murder of corrections officers. How many police officers have been killed in Connecticut? Not many.

And you think it's because of the death penalty?

I don't know. You can't say it is a deterrent. You can't say it *isn't* a deterrent. How do you know?

So why do we need a death penalty?

The reason we have it is because a majority of the people in the state of Connecticut, in fact a majority of the people in this country, want it. The legislature reinstated it. If anything, they continually strengthen it, right? In a democratic society, it's the legislature that makes the law. It's the will of the people. As prosecutors, it's our job to enforce the law.

If it's not necessarily a deterrent, what does the death penalty accomplish?

It's society's way of saying, "Hey, you've committed terrible, terrible crimes. As a punishment, we don't want you in society. We don't trust you in society."

So put them in jail.

What does that say to people who work in prisons? Let's say you're serving a life sentence without the possibility of release. What prevents you from popping the warden in the mouth, or beating up a prison guard, or killing a fellow prisoner?

We Can't Forget the Victims

By that logic, we wouldn't have life without the possibility of parole. We would just kill more people.

For some people [only]. When people talk about the death penalty, they never look at the victims, at the nature of the crime. I went to a death penalty seminar. . . . What they had was the seven people on death row. They had pictures blown up on the table. It had their names, their date of birth, and where they lived. The pictures were on a table so people coming in could look at them. I stood up and said, "Where are the pictures of the victims?"

If you think it's objectionable for people to look only at the humanity of the killers, aren't you making the same mistake in reverse—maybe not as seriously because they were innocent—by looking only at the humanity of the victims?

In fact, in these trials, the jury who's deciding whether or not the person deserves to die, they are looking at the humanity of the defendant. They're hearing everything about the defendant from day one. They never really hear about the victim other than to see the autopsy. The ultimate decision whether or not someone receives the death penalty, it's up to a jury or three judges.

But without John Connelly, it's not going to get there.

Right. To present the evidence. These cases are time-consuming.

You've got to be adamant to win them.

You have to persevere. The death penalty unit files all sorts of motions. They're not easy cases. I guess I could sit back and spend my time doing something else. But I'm here to do my job.

Nothing Personal

What if your son had gone wrong? What if instead of going to college, he got involved in drugs, got lost, freaked out, and killed somebody, and she was pregnant and the baby died. Would you want him to be killed?

Hopefully you're never in that situation. Who knows what you would do.

I'm not asking what you would do. You wouldn't be the prosecutor, obviously. Do you think the prosecutor should go for the death penalty? How would you feel?

I don't think it's a fair question.

Why's it an unfair question?

If somebody raped your wife and brutally murdered her, slit her throat, tortured her and raped her, gets up and says, "I'm glad I did it. I'm happy I did it." How would you feel?

I would want that person in jail forever.

How would you feel if in jail he raped a counselor? . . . I think it's unfair to personalize it. It's not personal. You're doing your job. People just look at the defendants. No one looks at the victims.

Witness to an Execution

Richard W. Byrne

On October 8, 1993, Andre Graham shot Sheryl Stack and her male companion as he stole Stack's car. Stack died two days later, and although her companion survived, he lost an eye and suffered brain damage. The next month Graham and his partner shot and killed a couple during a cocaine deal. His partner was executed for murdering the couple, and Graham received a life sentence plus twenty-three years for those murders. Graham was then sentenced to death for the murder of Sheryl Stack. He was executed on December 9, 1999.

Richard W. Byrne was a citizen witness to Graham's execution. He had no personal involvement with Graham or his victims. Rather, he volunteered to witness the execution as a learning experience, wondering if it would change his long-held pro–death penalty stance. In the end, Byrne left the death house with his initial beliefs intact. He realized that while he had mercy for Graham, he held no sympathy for him. Because Graham had chosen to take the lives of innocent people, Byrne concluded, he had also forfeited his own right to life.

Witness to an Execution

Impressions on the Execution of Andre Graham—12-09-99

It wasn't until I started home from work that it really started to hit me that, tonight, instead of watching the news and the Thursday night football game, I was going to go watch a man die. I was starting to get a little scared and thinking that maybe I was nuts for wanting to go through with this.

When I was working with behavior-disordered kids, some of whom were in the criminal justice system, I had thought it would be a valuable learning experience. Being a strong advocate of the death penalty, I had often wondered if my position would change were I to ever actually see an execution.

On this night, I was going to find out. I had an hour and a half drive to get there and plenty of time to think about what I was going to see.

Meeting the Other Witnesses

The witnesses met at the State Police station in Jarrett. We introduced ourselves to each other and I learned that the official witnesses had a long history of involvement with the object of the evening's exercise, Mr. Graham. They were a Commonwealth attorney, the man who prosecuted the case and officers or deputies who had been involved with the investigation, capture and conviction of the condemned man.

We were picked up and taken to the penitentiary by a representative of the Department of Corrections. There was joking and a little "gallows humor" on the way over which I found a little odd. A rather cold-hearted group, I thought. Once at the prison, we were taken to a holding area where the gentleman from DOC briefed us. The time was 7:35. An impressive and thorough professional, he carefully walked us through the events that were about to take place. Prior to this presentation, we had about 20 minutes to mill around and talk, drink coffee, etc. I was still feeling awkward and a little nervous.

I talked to one of the law enforcement officers and he told me of his long experience with Mr. Graham; a long history of serious crimes had included involvement in "at least ten killings that we know of for sure." I was told to make no mistake about it, this guy was "a cold blooded killer" and not someone who just happened to be "in the wrong place at the wrong time." To hear these guys talk about it, you didn't get any sense of blood lust or mindless vengeance at work, but a strong sense of people who were here to witness someone getting what they deserved. More than one made the comment that they had seen firsthand the human destruction that was left in the wake of Mr. Graham when he was free to roam the streets.

The Briefing

The briefing began at 7:50, and we were joined by two reporters, one male and one female, who turned out to be somewhat annoying. From the outset, their demeanor and the tone of their comments and questions left little doubt about the contempt that they felt for the whole process of which they were a part. During the briefing we were told what kind of a day the condemned man had. His final visit was with his mother, two sisters, two brothers and a stepfather. It began at about 1 o'clock and ended at 3:02. I thought to myself that when he said his goodbyes he had less than six hours to live.

Two curious things about this briefing were the matter of fact manner in which it was conducted and the irritating manner of the comments and questions of the reporters. I remember thinking to myself that these two were proof of the liberal bias of the media. They wanted to know who the other witnesses were and if any were members of law enforcement. We had all been introduced as just "citizen witnesses." Several times they would ask the group who they were and why they were there and at no time did I see one of the law enforcement people as much as acknowledge the question. I was asked and had no problem telling them. One seemed amazed, the other appalled that I would have volunteered to witness such an event.

A second question that seemed to obsess the male reporter was whether the prisoner was going to be given some type of drug to sedate him prior to the execution. Despite being told several times that being given a drug for that purpose was not a part of the execution process, he persisted with the question in at least 6 different versions and did everything but accuse the DOC rep of lying about it. The DOC rep never appeared irritated, even allowing the possibility that the prisoners' physician might prescribe something to him for medical reasons. But if that were the case, DOC would not be permitted to divulge such information. That wasn't good enough for the reporter and he seemed determined to prove his assumption that the condemned would be heavily sedated upon entering the execution chamber. Finally, our DOC man assured him that he had witnessed close to 60 executions and had never seen a condemned prisoner who wasn't completely alert and fully aware of what was going on. I thought of the quote that there is nothing like waiting to be executed to focus your concentration. The final question along this tedious line was to the effect of, "If he is not sedated, don't you think he should be, since this is supposed to be a humane exercise?"

It occurred to me that a good idea, and one that would have pleased the reporter, would be to institute a policy whereby condemned prisoners would be permitted to begin drinking martinis sometime before the execution—sort of a last happy hour. Liberals never seem to tire of reminding you of their superiority of character that is due to their infinite compassion. They also make it apparent the great depth of pity and contempt that they hold for those who are not so enlightened. Not surprisingly, there were no questions regarding the previous actions of Mr. Graham, which had led him to a point where he had less than an hour to live. The time was 8:15.

The Ride to the Death House

From this point on, things began to happen in an almost surreal manner. Events were moving rapidly but at the same time in a kind of slow motion. Prior to being frisked and loaded into the van for the short ride to the death house (that's what they called it), I noticed that my pulse had quickened and I had become hyper-alert to all that was going on around me.

During the ride to the maximum security area of the prison there was idle chatter among the other witnesses about the physical appearance of the prison that I thought was just weird. I personally thought it was the most eerie and depressing place I had ever seen. The bright lights, sterile buildings and miles of barbed wire made me feel as if I were on the set of some futuristic sci-fi movie.

As we pulled up to the gate, we drove past a van that was sitting just off to the side. The DOC man told us that van contained members of the victim's family who were here to witness the execution. As he was saying this, I was looking into the van and caught sight of an older woman who appeared to be wrapped in a blanket. I have never seen the look of such sadness and pain in the face of another human being.

I ran again quickly through my mind the details of the crime for which Mr. Graham was about to pay with his life. The facts had been given to me by the prosecuting attorney just a short time ago. They were brutal and chilling. Suffice it to say that because Mr. Graham and a partner needed a car one night, a 20 year old girl and a 22 year old boy ended up laying face down in a parking lot, each with a bullet in the back of their head. The boy had somehow survived, a cripple, but the girl had now been dead for over 6 years. In the back of that van, I got a 5 second glimpse at the anguish that will probably never go away for those poor, miserable souls.

Observations from the Witness Room

The van pulled up to the back of a small building. We entered and were searched with a metal detector and then led single file down a short hallway. A right turn, down another short hallway that led into a small room. Just before that room, on the left, was a doorway that led into a small room that we were escorted into. This room had windows running across the front of it and several rows of chairs. The first row of five chairs was up close to the glass. Elevated behind the first row was the second row of five chairs. I was the sixth one in the line so I had to take the first seat in the second row.

Before me was the unobstructed view of a small room. I was surprised at how small the area was. Almost directly in front of me, not more than ten or fifteen feet away, was the gurney. The foot of the gurney was pointed in the direction of our witness room and slightly to the right. Off to my right, perhaps 15 feet from the gurney, was a doorway with a clock above it. Next to the door was a man holding a red phone receiver—the direct line to the governor. Along the back of the room was stretched a blue curtain or tarpaulin, about two feet from the gurney which was perpendicular to it. There were three tiny windows in the curtain right above the head of the gurney. Three plastic tubes protruded from the curtain and extended out to the back of the gurney. My eyes also caught the sight of another large dark mirror to the right of the red phone. This was the one-way glass in front of the room from which the victim's family would witness the execution. The time was 8:45.

I noticed that I was sweating a little and my pulse had quickened. I was extremely alert. I remember thinking, "This is some serious shit!"

After taking our places in the witness room, the DOC man explained what was happening outside the door that the condemned man would be coming through in a few minutes. He had been kept in a holding cell just outside of that door for the last four days and was watched around the clock by guards who would be with him right up to the execution. They would explain to him what would be happening. He would be informed that barring a last minute stay of execution, this thing was going to happen and one way or another he would be strapped down to the gurney.

About 15 minutes prior to the scheduled execution, he would be handcuffed and taken out of the cell. There, the death warrant would be read to him. His attorney and a spiritual advisor would accompany him. He then would be led into the execution area. In that area, I was surprised at the number of people who were standing around. It was explained that they were DOC people, the warden, and several witnesses from the Commonwealth's Attorney's office. There were over a dozen people coming in and out of the room and standing around. Very little talking was going on.

The Execution Process Begins

At precisely five minutes to nine, I noticed that everyone in the room had stopped moving around. Suddenly the door opened to my right and two very large and muscular guards walked into the room. Behind them was the prisoner and the first sight of him was the most intense moment of the entire experience. I had tried to be prepared for this moment of looking into the eyes of someone who knew that in a few minutes he would be dead. I had anticipated that I would be looking into the eyes of fear and terror or eyes of intense sorrow and regret.

The prisoner was a well-built young black man with dreadlocks, wearing jeans and a denim shirt. The only restraints on him were handcuffs and if he wore ankle bracelets I did not notice them. I was staring intently at his eyes. What I saw was a look of hatred and contempt as he deliberately looked directly into the room where we were sitting. I remember thinking that the look was one of, "F--- you people," as he slowly shuffled toward the gurney.

In front of him were two guards, two were at his side and two were directly behind him. They looked like they had been recruited from the WWF [World Wrestling Federation]. After his brief glance into the witness room, he was quickly at the gurney and he turned to sit up and lay down. At that point he looked somewhat bewildered. I thought then that the DOC man was right; Mr. Graham was alert and fully aware of everything that was going on around him. As he laid himself onto the gurney, each guard was in position to begin fastening the thick leather straps to his body.

After the straps were secured, one guard walked around the gurney to check the straps while the others stood around the gurney, almost at attention. When this was done the guards exited to my left from the room. I noticed that one of the guards was obviously stressed out by the situation. As he exited the room, he was biting his lip and had the look of someone who was about to break down in tears. Other than that guard, it was striking how smoothly and efficiently this entire process was being played out. There were no awkward movements from any of the participants, no moments when someone appeared to be uncertain about what to do next.

Thinking of the Victim

At that point, a curtain was pulled across the front of the windows as the intravenous lines were hooked up to the prisoner. It was at this point that I bowed my head to say a prayer for the condemned. I then thought of the murdered twenty-year-old girl and said a short prayer for her and the anguished members of her family. I thought of what one of the attorneys had told me. She had been a part-time college student, young, attractive, at the beginning of her life. And it had been ended for no good reason. And over six years had passed since then. Six years of joys and hopes and experiences that she and her loved ones would never have.

I thought of myself, and what I was doing here as witness to this vast human tragedy. I had mercy for the guy lying on the other side of the curtain, but I had no sympathy. I realized then that what I was witnessing was not going to change me into an opponent of the death penalty.

I also had a surge of contempt for the reporters sitting to my right and the media they represented.

How many times had I read articles about death penalty cases in which the victim barely receives a mention, as if they are an irritating and inconsequential sidelight to the whole story in a capital punishment case? Discussion of the victim of course destroys any possible strength and validity that the usual specious and empty-headed arguments against the death penalty might have.

I Watched the Last Breath

Only a couple of minutes had passed when the curtain was drawn open before us. Again I was aware of the "slow motion" effect, as seconds moved by as if minutes and senses strained to absorb every detail of the macabre scene that was unfolding several feet in front of me. I had noticed that from the time Mr. Graham laid on the gurney, he stared straight up at the ceiling. My position of observation was somewhat above him so that I could see his eyes as they blinked. He never turned his head to look left or right.

As the curtain was drawn back, a man was leaning down and talking rapidly to Mr. Graham, only inches from his face. Graham never looked at him. This was his spiritual advisor. He finished speaking, Mr. Graham nodded twice, and the man turned and walked away. He entered the room where I was sitting and sat in the back row. Several seconds after he left, the warden, who was standing a couple of feet away from Mr. Graham's head, stepped up to the gurney and said, "Do you have any final words to say?" Mr. Graham said nothing audible and made no motion with his head.

The warden stepped back and immediately nodded to someone standing to the right of the gurney. That person in turn nodded in the direction of the openings in the curtain behind the head of the prisoner. As you watched the tubes leading from the curtain, you could see one start to slightly jiggle.

I fixed my eyes on Mr. Graham. His eyes were blinking more rapidly than they had been. He didn't appear to be breathing hard but he was taking deep breaths. He took two deep breaths. His eyes fluttered, blinked a couple more times and then softly closed. His chest raised with a breath several more times. At that point, the most obvious thing that I was aware of was an oppressive silence that could be felt. I have never experienced a comparable silence. A pin dropping would have sounded like glass shattering.

I watched the last breath and his chest moved no more. The warden came from behind the curtain (I hadn't noticed him leave) and said something to a man standing there that I couldn't make out. Our DOC man turned to us and said, "The time of death was 9:04." I shot a glance at the clock on the wall. From the time Mr. Graham had walked through that door to pronouncement of death, nine minutes had elapsed. After another couple of minutes the curtain closed. We were then told that we would return to the vans and be taken to our cars. It was over.

Sorting Out My Feelings

After getting back into the van, several of the deputies and attorneys had comments. The first comment was, "I'm sorry. But for what he did, that sonovabitch got off easy." I asked the deputy sitting next to me what he thought of the prisoner's expression when he walked through the door. He said that he was a mean, heartless bastard right up to the end. No remorse. I asked another if he had ever had occasion to talk to Mr. Graham since he had arrested him. He said no, but he was in the court the day he was sentenced to death. As the prisoner was led away their eyes met and the officer looked at him, pulled the trigger of an imaginary gun, and blew the smoke from the barrel. He intended, he said, to convey the message that, "We GOT you this time, baby!"

There was one other question that I wanted an answer to. Why had none of these men acknowledged the several attempts by the reporters to question them? One spoke for them all and said that they had learned a long time ago that if you say anything to a reporter, your words would be twisted to suit the purpose of the reporter, and would have little similarity to their original meaning. The best way to deal with reporters was to not even respond to their questions. It was surprising how quickly the conversations changed to more mundane matters such as their current jobs or what was happening in this or that case. After the short ride back to the police barracks, I shook hands with the people I had met and got into my car to drive home.

The ride home gave me over an hour to sort out my thoughts and feelings. It was an awful thing that I had just witnessed. The intensity, the gravity of it was draining. I had been increasingly apprehensive about being a witness as the time drew near. I thought that I might well see something that would change my support of the death penalty.

Years ago I was an opponent of the death penalty and had subscribed to the many arguments against its use. It is inhumane, not worthy of a civilized society. The wrong person might be executed. No other advanced society continues to execute, only countries like Iran or Communist China. It is given unfairly, only to the poor and minorities. There is no evidence that it is a deterrent. It is legalized murder by the state, little different than the act of the criminal, (the most absurd of all the arguments). A life sentence serves the purpose just as well.

And on and on go the tired arguments from watery intellects that appeal to emotion over reason. I grow more conservative with age and many of the views I hold today I would have considered ridiculous twenty years ago. I read somewhere once that any man who at the age of 18 is not a liberal has no heart; and any man who at the age of 35 is not a conservative has no mind. I think of that quote whenever I hear a liberal argue about anything, especially the death penalty.

Justice Was Served

The death penalty is just. What good is a society that does not proclaim the right to life as one of the ultimate values? A person who wantonly takes the life of an innocent human being should pay the ultimate price, if the sacredness of life is to have any meaning at all.

The focus should be on the life of the innocent and the death penalty a statement by society that for certain acts, a person forfeits any right to a life of their own. Life is sacred, and despite the liberal mindset that abhors passing judgments or making distinctions between good and evil, the value of an innocent life over one of a cold blooded murderer must be acknowledged.

It is not the death penalty that cheapens life or makes the society that employs it barbaric. There was nothing barbaric about the execution of Mr. Graham. What is barbaric, as well as tragic and pitiful, is the thinking that fails to make the distinction between the life of Mr. Graham and the life of the young girl he was responsible for ending. It is the society that fails to make that distinction, in a way that is dramatic and without equivocation, which is truly the barbaric one.

Voices of Families Touched by the Death Penalty

I Am a Death Row Wife

Saffiya S. Musaaleh

In 1998 Saffiya S. Musaaleh became the pen pal of Patrick Boni-fay (now known as Nabiyl Musaaleh), an inmate on Florida's death row, and the two were subsequently married. In the fol-lowing selection, Saffiya describes her relationship with Nabiyl and his family and recounts her efforts to prevent her husband's execution.

Nabiyl had been sentenced to death for a 1990 murder that he had committed at the age of seventeen. In 2005 the U.S. Su-preme Court deemed it cruel and unusual punishment to ex-ecute those convicted of murders committed prior to the age of eighteen. Therefore, Nabiyl will now be eligible for parole after serving twenty-five years.

Saffiya Musaaleh agrees with the Supreme Court's ruling, ar-guing that juveniles should not be executed because they possess neither the emotional nor the social maturity that would make them responsible for their crimes. She goes on to assert that the death penalty takes away a person's ability to change and to be-come a rehabilitated member of society.

I Am a Death Row Wife

I have been a Death Row 'wife' for the past seven years. Though many believe that the Death Penalty affects only the man or woman sentenced to die in the most egregious of ways, it certainly affects the wife or husband, and other family members left at home. As a (soon to be former) Death Row 'wife', I am fortunate; due to the Supreme Court's ruling [*Roper v. Simmons*], my husband, Nabiyl Musaaleh, will be removed from DR in a short time. I have prayed for this day, always believing my husband's life had a purpose.

Saffiya S. Musaaleh, "My Views on the Death Penalty,". www.deathrowspeaks.com. Re-produced by permission.

I never thought about the Death Penalty in any aspect before 1996; I had lived a full life, served in the military, attended college, and enjoyed family and friends. In 1997 or there so, my brother gave me a book written by Death Row inmate Mumia Abu-Jamal. Its title, *Live from Death Row*. I read it from cover to end, intrigued, questioning the saneness of a system that sought to imprison unlawfully. Abu-Jamal's predicament spoke to me in that I had served this country and experienced a control that sought to undermine me, to take away my freedom. I learned to fight against that system, much like Abu-Jamal did through his powerful essays.

He Was Someone I Had to Meet

In 1998, I was online seeking to write a pen pal, possibly from another country and by chance, I came across an ad that was my Nabiyl's. It was a page from the PrisonPenPals.com site, and I read it and tried to make out the picture that was his. I couldn't tell what my husband looked like; the picture was too dark to discern his features. I just knew that he was someone I had to meet. I did not hesitate to write him. Within a few weeks, I had a reply. From that point on, we wrote, sharing ideas, beliefs, and goals for the future. A future that might find me without him as a friend.

It is a common fact that when we love someone on the inside, we don't look at what they have done in the past, better yet, what they may have done to arrive at their station in life does not faze us because we see into their hearts. We see the changes they have made to better themselves. On Death Row, this is the only thing a man can do, for solitude envelops him, and allows him reflection.

Another common thing, for one on Death Row, is they lose contact with the outside world. Family drops away, either from distance and dealing with their daily lives, or because separation is better, disassociation helps to mend fences with a society that decided the sentenced man or woman was better off condemned. This separation is so final, and it is the harshest aspect of confinement on the Row. It leaves one there feeling desolate, without hope, knowing loneliness.

He Deserved Another Chance

In the case of my husband, he was sentenced to Death Row at the age of 17; this was 1990. I worked as an educator at the time I met my husband, and understood that a juvenile acts and processes life differently than an adult. To quit things undertaken, to believe in immortality, to see only as far as the night's outcome, is their capacity. My husband was such a youth, his ideals at the time shaped by the streets that claimed him. His path a product of a home life that did not allow him a blueprint for success as my own had. Knowing this helped me form my opinion about Death Row/the Death Penalty. I believed in my heart that my husband deserved another chance; that the state of Florida needed to look at his case again, and grant him life, if nothing more. Every letter to my husband promoted these thoughts, and when I began to visit him, the moments before leaving were tear-filled because of this resolve. Eventually, I learned to be strong and the tears stopped, prayers took over, and I waited.

While I waited, I researched, looked at law, read and prayed he would be spared his life. I grew closer to his family, and by doing so opened an avenue that allowed some healing between them, that closed a rift to the greater extent. My husband will attest to this, and though he feels there are patterns to the life his family lives that he cannot alter, he knows he wants to help them see a future different than what might be if he should ever get out.

The Death Penalty for Juveniles

And what my opinion is on the Death Penalty is the question at hand. In March 2003, I believe, my husband and I did separate interviews with a German television station. A question was asked of me regarding how I felt about the Death Penalty in regards to juveniles.

My answer (then and currently): To say a young man or lady is not worthy of rehabilitation is wrong. They can change; can become productive members of society if given the chance. We build more prisons with the goal of locking up anyone who is incorrigible in lieu of society's standards. We fail to build and revamp schools. The problem is that education is devalued and killing is lauded where our young people are concerned. Yes, they have done wrong, taken a life, harmed someone, taken a family's loved one away; however, what are the factors that put them there? What hand does society play when we look at government spending, at the lack of available social service programs for the mother struggling to raise a family of too many children and few employment opportunities? Blame it on the country, the state, and the county? Not fully, but collectively will suffice. Each has played a hand in the demise of our youth one way or the other. Each is culpable for failing to implement a safety net that would have quelled loss on all sides, I believe.

We Should Stop the Killing Field

There is a memory I hold in my heart where my husband's time on Death Row is concerned. He and I are soulmates, hearts that came together when time allowed our union. My husband and I were working on a project together. I had stopped writing for a week, to reassess the writing process. Sitting in my living room, I experienced a sadness, an overwhelming feeling that he was experiencing loss. I could only ride the feeling out, could only pray that he would feel better. On a visit thereafter, I learned that a good friend of his had been executed, dragged away to a finality that would separate him from the life granted him. From friends, such as my husband, that had helped him know compassion where before it was absent.

I held him, and in my heart prayed that I would not know that loss.

The Death Penalty allows any state that fosters it, a killing field, and a license to be God. It is finality, and by all means necessary should be quelled.

We have seen innocent men freed from the row, have read about botched executions that registered the inhumanity of this system.

The Death Penalty is truly an end to life's possibility.

The possibility of change to one condemned before.

Thank you for taking the time to read this, and my prayers are with everyone who has to live with the knowledge their loved one might be put to death.

The Execution of My Mentally Ill Brother

Catherine Forbes

On January 10, 1984, Thomas Provenzano entered Florida's Orange County Courthouse armed with a revolver, a shotgun, and an assault rifle. He opened fire, leaving one man dead at the scene and two others paralyzed (one of the paralyzed men died seven years later). Provenzano was tried for murder and was eventually executed in 2000.

The following selection was written by Provenzano's sister, Catherine Forbes. She contends that her brother should not have been executed for his crime because he was mentally ill and therefore should not be held completely responsible for his actions. Indeed, under U.S. law, a defendant can be found not guilty by reason of insanity if it can be established that he was too mentally ill to be fully aware of his actions or to know the difference between right and wrong. According to Forbes, her brother met this description because he believed he was Jesus and that there was a conspiracy against him.

Should the Mentally Ill Be Executed?

I don't quite know where to begin, but I have a need and a responsibility to tell my story on how the State of Florida wrongfully executed my brother. He was executed on June 22nd, 2000. His name was Thomas Provenzano and he meant the world to me. Thomas was mentally ill and was incompetent to be executed. Even though it was proved that Thomas was mentally ill, "they" said he was competent to be executed. Think about that: competent enough to be killed. Thomas' illness began with headaches, and then his entire personality changed. I tried to get help, but we could not afford private

Catherine Forbes, "The Execution of a Mentally Ill Man," www.celldoor.com, 2000. Reproduced by permission.

hospitalization. Without Thomas' permission, I could get help only if he did something violent. When he did become violent, however, "help" came in the form of a death sentence.

He Believed That He Was Jesus

Thomas believed that he was Jesus since the early seventies. The incident was committed in 1984. He even got mad at me for letting my son have much needed thyroid surgery because he said he healed him. There were many incidents like that one. Once he held his picture up to Jesus and said, "What do you see? It's me isn't it?" The point I am trying to make is he was in a very bad way and yet they still put him through a trial and sentenced him to death. What they should have done was put him in a hospital where he belonged for so many years. Americans need to invest in true intervention programs, so people can get help for loved ones who are mentally ill before they harm themselves or an innocent person. If treatment had been available for Thomas, he would be alive today and so would the three people he harmed. He didn't fully understand his crime because he thought it was a conspiracy to get Jesus. Seven Florida Supreme Court Judges all agreed that he truly believed that he was Jesus.

So at the time of that fatal injection who did they murder, Jesus or Thomas? We'll never know, will we? I wasn't even able to have a last phone call with him that day. The warden denied me that last wish. Because Thomas believed he was Jesus he couldn't, of course, prepare for his death. I know he felt he would be back in another form, because he said, "They can only get my body."

A Mentally Ill Man on Death Row

The night before an execution is an unimaginable nightmare. I had to go through that three times. The State of Florida chose to make me and my family victims too, despite the alternatives that existed. The public has a right to know how they treat our mentally ill in prisons all across America. My brother slept with a handmade mask over his mouth every day and night. He didn't want the demons or voices to enter his body. At night he would holler at them to show themselves so he could kill them! He often even strapped a cardboard box around his back and slept under his bunk. Thomas did this for sixteen years! I can't believe this was allowed to go on so long and no one cared. This became normal behavior for Thomas. I didn't have a clue how he was being treated until the end when it came out in court. When I heard of how they let him suffer like that and for so long I died inside and I'm still dying inside.

Our Whole Family Suffered

To me Thomas falls in the category of an innocent child not knowing what he did and not fully understanding what he was accused of doing. It makes him INNOCENT! So I can, without any reservations, accuse the State of Florida of taking an innocent life! There is so much more to my brother's story and I pray to God that I can do something to reach as many people as I can to make them aware just how bad our Justice System truly is. I know there are others out there going through what Thomas and his family went through. The public only sees or hears about us on the eve of an execution. Of course we are crying and our hearts are about to be broken and that's all they see. If the normal human being that believes in the death penalty can walk in our shoes for just one day it might change a few minds. That's why I would so much like to write a step by step piece on the last sixteen years of my brother's incarceration.

There was no outpouring of support for the family of the condemned. In fact my children were beaten at school when their uncle was convicted as "a murderer." We did nothing wrong, but we were certainly punished. How can a society that despises violent crime so easily dismiss its own violent acts of retribution? The death of a loved one is always a terrible experience—particularly in the case of murder. But losing a loved one to execution is also a terrible experience that is virtually ignored by our society. Does this indifference somehow make executions more tolerable? The death penalty is a deliberate but avoidable act of homicide that always leaves a grieving family in its wake. Thomas's cause of death says just that: homicide!!!! If this reaches and changes one person's belief in executions then I can honestly say I made a difference.

Thomas Was Mentally Incompetent

I would also like to mention that all the doctors that evaluated Thomas also found him to be incompetent, including Dr. Lyons, who was one of the most prominent of all. He was the doctor that came up with the Post War Syndrome. One of the doctors that Tommy saw before the incident who found him to be in a paranoid state was later one of the doctors used to testify for the State at time of trial. How ironic is that? Of course he said Thomas was sane enough to stand trial because he worked in that courtroom and for the State quite frequently. Even the three doctors the state hired conceded at the end that Tommy truly believed he was Jesus. He didn't rationally understand but he factually understood why he was being put to death. But remember Thomas thought the whole story was made up to get Jesus so he really didn't factually understand either.

Thomas was like a parrot. He would repeat everything someone told him. I would repeat things over and over to him until I felt he got it and could repeat it back. I still wanted to believe that I could get through to him and hoped that one day he would be normal and we could have a good conversation. But that never happened. When he would repeat conversations or some fifty dollar word that he heard they thought he was faking it. I had to take the stand at one of his hearings, by my suggestion to his lawyer, to clear up a statement that he made. He told someone that the jury vacillated in their decision about him. Thomas had no clue what that meant. He just repeated what I said. It was just like someone who is in a coma. You speak to them hoping that you are getting through.

That's how it was for me with Thomas. I spoke normally to him always. But I always agreed with him even if it was wrong. I had to do this so he didn't think I was part of the conspiracy. At one time he did and he wouldn't speak to me for years, so I couldn't take that chance again. The prosecutor tried to trick me on the stand and jeopardize my relationship with Tommy at the end. He asked me straight out in front of Tommy if I thought Thomas was Jesus. I looked at Thomas and said, "My brother doesn't lie, sir, and if he says he is Jesus then that's who he is. Besides I've never seen anyone that said they were Jesus so how do I know he isn't?"

Dr. Fleming was there at the time and she thought that was a great response especially for Thomas. Dr. Fleming was another doctor that played a big part in trying to show overwhelming evidence of Thomas's incompetence. I believe the records are public record for anyone to read so if you ever get a chance to read his files you will see just how overwhelming is the proof of his incompetence to be executed.

A Mother's Journey to Forgiveness

Aba Gayle

In 1980 Catherine Blount was staying at her friend Eric's home when Eric's friend, Douglas Mickey, stopped by for a visit. There was nothing noteworthy about that night; the three had dinner together and even played a board game. But later in the evening a fight broke out between the two men, and Mickey stabbed both Eric and Catherine to death.

For eight long years Catherine's mother, Aba Gayle, was consumed by the desire for revenge as she waited for the execution that she thought would bring closure to her pain. Then, in 1988 she began studying and meditating on forgiveness as a way of life. That practice led her in 1992 to write a letter expressing her forgiveness to Douglas Mickey. As soon as the letter was sent, Gayle claims she was filled with peace and found healing for the grief that had consumed her for so long. She has since developed a friendship with Mickey that she continues to this day, and has established the Catherine Blount Foundation to help others find peace through forgiveness.

Teaching the Healing Power of Forgiveness

By all definitions I am a victim for I am the mother of a beautiful young daughter who was brutally murdered. But I have learned that there is another way to live and that I have a choice. I have chosen to stop being a victim. This has not been an easy road to travel!

My story began one early fall day in 1980 with a phone call. The voice at the other end of the line said, "Well, what do you think about Catherine being shot?"

I said, "What do you mean? What are you talking about?"

"Well, haven't you heard? Catherine was shot!"

I quickly got off the phone and called the sheriff's department and said, "This is Gayle, mother of Catherine Blount. I hear she has been shot. Where is she? How is she? I must go to her!"

The voice at the other end of the line was obviously embarrassed to have to talk to me. He said, "No, ma'am your daughter hasn't been shot. Your daughter is dead. I will have Sheriff Landry call you right back."

Going Insane

I now know what it is like to be insane. All I could do was wait for the phone to ring. My body was tense and tight and there was a tingling pain all over. I paced and drank tea and waited for the phone to ring. Finally, after three long hours, I could wait no longer and called the sheriff's department again. I simply said, "Someone must speak to me because I'm losing my mind." Finally, Detective Landry came on the line. He was as kind and gentle as possible as he spoke these terrible words to me. "I'm sorry, but your daughter, Catherine, is dead. Your daughter was murdered. She was stabbed to death."

Something in my heart broke. My brain couldn't think. I had to remain calm. None of this day was real. Soon I would wake up and the nightmare would be over. But deep down inside, I knew it was real. I couldn't let anyone hug me, I was afraid I would break down. I couldn't cry, someone might hear me. I decided to take a shower and with the water running full blast, I screamed and screamed and screamed.

My Time of Darkness

This was the start of a period of 8 years I now call "my time of darkness."

In order to survive in this life you just do what you have to do to keep your head above water. My method of survival was to be calm and not cause anyone any problems. I had no support system. I had no faith. I did not believe in God. I didn't have a minister, a priest or a rabbi, or anyone who could comfort me and help me. I had to remain strong to help everyone else.

My mother was recovering from open-heart surgery and she was very fragile. I had to protect her from my pain; I couldn't allow her to see how much I was suffering. My son and daughter had just left for medical school; I couldn't burden them with my tears—they had enough to do to put aside their own pain as they began four years of grueling medical training. My husband announced that he didn't want to talk about Catherine any more; he stated emphatically that he did not intend to mourn her the rest of his life. I found myself more and more isolated with no one to give me the love and encouragement I needed so badly. For a while, I could not even drive my car alone because, when I was alone, I would cry and I couldn't see the road.

On the surface, I carried on the false front. Had you known me at that time, you wouldn't have known about the dark, ugly cloud I carried around inside me. You would have thought I was getting along just fine. But, inside of me, a deep, dark rage began to boil. There was this awful, hideous darkness, and all I wanted was revenge for the death of my beloved child.

The District Attorney told me that the sheriff's department would find the person who murdered Catherine. The District Attorney would put him on trial, get a guilty conviction, and make certain that the murderer would receive the death penalty. (Douglas Mickey was arrested, tried, convicted and sentenced to death in 1982.) I was assured that when that horrible villain was executed, I would be healed of my pain and all would be well again. And, because I didn't know any other way to believe, I thought that was true!

The Healing Begins

After eight long years of a passionate lust for revenge, I un-knowingly began my first step toward healing. I began taking a course in meditation. After a time, I found myself able to sit quietly, to be still in my head, and to be in the present moment. For the first time in my life, I realized that I did not have to see, touch or even hear something to know that it is real. I learned there is far more to this Universe than our senses perceive.

My mother's failing health left her quite fragile. I was blessed at this time to be able to live with and care for her. I was always looking for ways to help her enjoy the highest quality of life possible. One way I chose to do this was to take her to church. I found a beautiful little Unity Church in Auburn, CA. The church was a 20-minute drive from our home through beautiful country. This church helped me change my life and find my God-self.

I discovered the church's bookstore. Here I found books on Christianity, Buddhism, Hinduism, mythology and other books on the lives and teachings of the great religious and philosophical teachers who have come to this earth for our enlightenment. I started reading and studying my way through that bookstore. I learned I am a beloved child of God; I am one with the Universe; and all of us are here to love each other, without exception. God is a loving God and there is no hell except that which we create in our own minds. I really "got it" that we are *all One in Spirit.*

I was introduced to the book, *A Course in Miracles* by my minister, Reverend Billie Blaine. It was while watching a video introducing *A Course in Miracles* that I got my first glimpse of the Healing Power of Forgiveness. The video showed several interviews with people who studied *A Course In Miracles.* One of the men interviewed was Jewish and a holocaust survivor. He was able to forgive not only the German people, but the actual guards in the camps who had killed every member of his family. Something in me really clicked when I heard that testimony. I began to feel perhaps I could forgive the man who killed Catherine. A seed was planted in my heart.

A Letter to My Daugher's Killer

My mom and I moved to Santa Rosa to be closer to my daughter and grandchildren. I continued attending a study group for *The Course in Miracles*. Because the study group met in the same building, I also began attending the *Santa Rosa Church of Religious Science* and began taking classes to study "The Science of the Mind" by Ernest Holmes. My teachers were Rev. Mary Murry Shelton and Rev. Karyl Huntley. We spent a lot of time discussing forgiveness.

One day I received a letter from a friend in Auburn with a newspaper clipping stating that Douglas Mickey's execution was scheduled. I immediately called San Quentin and demanded that I be allowed to be a witness. I discovered the newspaper had made a mistake; there was no execution scheduled on the date stated. However, I was instructed to write a letter to the warden and request I be notified when there was a date set for Mickey's execution. This I did. I put the letter to the warden on my desk and prepared to go to class. That letter never did get mailed.

After many hours of study, prayer, and discussions with others, I thought that perhaps I could forgive the man who murdered Catherine. Perhaps, it would relieve my own frustration and suffering. That evening when a classmate suggested that I should let the murderer know of my intent. I was outraged!

Still feeling out of sorts at class that night because of the idea suggested by my classmate, I had a feeling of nervous expectation. Then, as I drove home from class, I distinctly heard a voice. It said to me, *"YOU MUST FORGIVE HIM AND YOU MUST LET HIM KNOW!"* This voice was so loud and so clear and so persuasive that I didn't sleep at all that night. I was literally impelled to get out of bed at four a.m. to type a letter to the man who murdered Catherine. The letter follows:

Dear Mr. Mickey

Twelve years ago, I had a beautiful daughter named Catherine. She was a young woman of unusual talents and intelligence. She was slender and her skin glowed with health and vitality. She had long naturally wavy hair that framed her sparkling eyes and warm bright smile. She radiated love and joy!

Catherine was living with her friend, Eric, on a fifteen-acre pear ranch. Catherine's greatest love was her animals. She was raising two milk goats, her German shepherd with a new litter of ten puppies and an Arabian mare. She had tried to live with her father and his wife on their property (where there would be room for all her animals), but her stepmother's emotional illness made that impossible and she had just recently moved back with her friend Eric.

Two months after her 19th birthday Catherine left her earthly body and her spirit transitioned to her next stage of life. I know that Catherine is in a better place than we can ever know here on earth. I did not know that when Catherine died. I knew that I had been robbed of my precious child and that she had been robbed of growing into womanhood and achieving all of her potential. The violent way she left this earth was impossible for me to understand. I was saddened beyond belief and felt that I would never be completely happy again. And indeed my loss of Catherine became the point of reference for my entire family. All family history was prefaced as happening either before or after Catherine's death.

I was very angry with you and wanted to see you punished to the limit of the law. You had done irreparable damage to my family and my dreams for the future.

After eight long years of grief and anger I started my journey of life. I met wonderful teachers and slowly began to learn about my God-self. In the midst of a class studying *A Course in Miracles* I was surprised to find that I could forgive you. This does not mean that I think you are innocent or that you are blameless for what happened. What I learned is this: You are a divine child of God. You carry the Christ consciousness within you. You are surrounded by God's love even as you sit in your cell. There is no devil; there is only the goodness of God. The Christ in me sends blessings to the Christ in you.

Do not look to me to be a political or social advocate in your behalf. The law of the land will determine your fate. Do not waste your last days on earth with remorse and fear. Death as we know it is really a new beginning. Hell does not exist except in our conscious minds.

I hope that this letter will help you to face your future. There is only love and good in the world regardless of how things may appear to you now. I am willing to write to you or visit you if you wish. I send blessings to you and to your children.

Gayle, Mother of Catherine

A State of Grace

I mailed this letter after receiving hugs of encouragement from my classmates in The Science of Mind Foundations Class. I can still feel the shivers going up and down my spine as I remember the little click that the hinged mailbox made as I dropped in this letter. When I heard that "click," all the anger, all the rage, all the lust for revenge—simply vanished in that instant. In its place I was filled with the most incredible feeling of Joy and Love and Peace. I was in A State of Grace. I knew in that Holy Instant I did not need to have anyone executed for me to be healed. I could now get on with my life!

It would not have mattered if Douglas Mickey responded to my letter. I had received a more profound answer. I had been healed by the simple act of *offering the gift* of forgiveness. However, I did get a letter back. I was totally amazed at the gentleness and kindness of the writer. Douglas wrote back with words of gratitude. He expressed remorse and sorrow for the crime, also stating that he fully understood how empty such words might sound. I could tell from reading his letter that he was intelligent and well-read. He had obviously spent years studying for answers himself. He wrote back, "The Christ in me most gratefully accepts and returns blessings of Divine Wisdom, Love and Charity to the Christ in you." He also said, "I would gladly give my life this instant if it would in any way change that terrible night."

Mickey enclosed a visiting form. It took 90 days to get permission from San Quentin to visit.

Facing Catherine's Killer

The very first time I was even near a prison or jail was when I visited Douglas in the visiting room at San Quentin California State Prison. . . .

When I arrived, in the visiting room for death row inmates I looked around with surprise. I did not see a single monster in that room. It was filled with ordinary looking men. (Perhaps neater and quieter than outside.) They were sitting with their grandmothers, or wives or ministers and/or their children. Everywhere I looked, I saw "The face of God."

When Douglas came in, he said, "Gayle, you do me the greatest honor by paying me this visit." We talked together for over three hours. I cried and he cried. We cried together. He is a big, tall, very strong man and he wasn't the least bit embarrassed to sit there, surrounded by other inmates, and openly weep. We talked about Catherine. We talked about Douglas's mother and her death. We talked about his losses. I realized the night Catherine lost her life, Douglas also lost his future.

A New Direction for My Grief

When I left San Quentin that day, after only one visit, I knew that I would never stop spreading the word that these men were human beings and not monsters. I knew that I would be a political and social advocate on their behalf. And, I knew that if the State of California ever executes Douglas Mickey, they would be killing my friend.

I now refer to the time I spend visiting men on death row as my "mini prison ministry." When asked by reporters if any of the men on death row have committed crimes which are just too awful for me to still treat them with compassion, I respond, "I don't deal with their crime. I don't deal with that part of them. I deal with the God spirit within him or her. That is the truth of their being. It is the truth for every one of us."

Before Catherine's murder, I had never thought one way or another about the death penalty. I was a Kappa Kappa Gamma at the University of Wisconsin, raised to be an upper middle-class housewife. My mother certainly didn't raise me to go visit men on death row. For most of the twelve years after Catherine was killed, I would have been insulted if someone had suggested that Douglas Mickey was a human being and not some kind of horrible monster.

I knew when I dropped the letter in the mailbox I must spend the rest of my life demonstrating that killing is not necessary and that violence only begets more violence. What I learned is healing and grace can be achieved by anyone under any circumstance through the miracle of forgiveness. This may have appeared to be a new paradigm to me as I began this healing journey, but it is actually the universal truth that has been given to all people through sacred teachings such as those expressed by Jesus, The Christ, the Buddha and other enlightened beings.

I know my daughter Catherine is happy I am honoring her with this work. She would not want me to go through life full of hate and rage. Love and forgiveness is the way to make our world a kind and safe place.

A Mother Speaks
for the Victims

Elizabeth Harvey, interview by PBS

The following selection is excerpted from an interview with Elizabeth Harvey conducted by the Public Broadcasting Service's program Frontline. *Harvey's daughter Faith was brutally raped and murdered in 1980 by Robert Lee Willie and Joseph Vacarro. Willie, who was convicted of the crime and was executed by electrocution on December 28, 1984, was the subject of Sister Helen Prejean's book* Dead Man Walking.

In the interview Harvey discusses her daughter's life and murder. She states that Willie received the punishment he deserved. Due to the barbarity of the crime, she insists, life in prison would have been too lenient. Harvey now attends every execution at Louisiana's Angola State Penitentiary, supporting the death penalty as a silent voice for crime victims.

A Voice for the Victims

Where was Faith that night . . . what was she doing?

Harvey: She left and went to work at the restaurant. She was covering for a girl that had covered for her while she was on her senior trip. She had final exams at school the next day. So they had swapped times. And then she went to tell some friends goodbye and went to the Lake Front Disco, where one of her classmates was a disc jockey for the sound system down there that night at a fashion show.

What was she about to do with her life?

Harvey: She was fixing to go into the Army. She had entered the summer before on the delayed entry program and her recruiting sergeant had called her on July the 18th in 1979.

And said, "Are you ready? Let's go sign." And she said, "No, today is my mother's birthday. I'm going to spend it with her. I'll go tomorrow." And I thought well what a thing in history to remember on my birthday, but it was though she had some premonition that she would never spend another birthday with me. And she completely refused to go that day.

What kind of girl was she?

Harvey: She enjoyed life very much. She didn't meet a stranger, she got to have a lot of animals. She's had rabbits, horses, she used to belong to the Mandeville Saddle Club. We've had squirrels and we raised dogs and I had some poodles that were born on her last birthday that she was alive.

It Leaves a Great, Big Void

What effect has it had on you and as a family, when something like what happened to Faith . . .?

Harvey: It leaves a great big void. It's a great big empty hole that is always there. It's something that you never believe it will happen. It's just such a shock that it's hard for your mind to a) accept a process that this is actually happening to me. I don't know where my loved one is. And my first born for the first time in my life I could say I didn't know where she was. It was extremely hard to believe that this was happening to me.

When you found out what happened . . .?

Harvey: Denial. I didn't want to believe that that was her. I told them prove it. I know what you've told me that has happened to this body. I don't wish it on anybody else. But prove to me that this is my daughter.

And they did?

Harvey: No, it took my own brother to finally come down to identify her and it was something that was extremely hard for him to do is to identify his niece and it was his first niece and they had become quite close.

I Never Saw Any Remorse

Robert Lee Willie and Joe Vaccaro were captured and there was a trial. What was your sense about them?

Harvey: Unbelievable—I couldn't understand how they could a done something so heinous, cruel and vindictive on another human being and you looked at them and they didn't look any different than anybody else. It was just something that wakes up your mind that it could be anybody out there that was doing these things and there's no way to know that. There's no way of distincting one from the other. There's nothing different about them at all.

And was there any way you could see that there could be redemption, that you could forgive them in some way for what happened?

Harvey: I never saw any remorse from them. I sat there all through the pre-trial hearings, the trials, the appeals. And I looked for any remorse or anything whatsoever that they could have been sorry for some of the crimes that they had committed because they had been on a crime spree. And never saw anything. They just—they made me feel like if they got a chance to do it again that that's what they would do.

You later learned—what were Faith's last words to them that you know and their last words to her?

Harvey: Herb Alexander, the prosecuting attorney's opening statement to the jury in Robert Willie's case, said that Faith's last words on this first was, "Please go away, leave me alone, let me die by myself." And the last words that Faith heard on this first was, "This bitch won't die. Die bitch. Die."

A Victim Has No Voice

Some people make the argument for life imprisonment and talk about rights that these condemned men have. How do you feel about that?

Harvey: If they got a life sentence they could talk to their family on the telephone, they could visit with them, they can see 'em at holidays, they can visit with them at Christmas time. Christmas time my chair is still empty at my table. To go visit Faith, I have to go to the grave. She can't come—I can't talk to her. I can't put my arms around her. A condemned man can get all of that if he spends his life in prison and I think he gave up that right whether it was a man or whether it was a woman. I think they gave up that right when they committed that—the day that they committed the crime.

So you feel comfortable with the death penalty as punishment. . . . Tell me how you come to that thinking.

Harvey: Well it's on the books and it's the law. And if you don't want to be executed then don't commit the crime. It's that simple. You can decide whether you commit that crime or not but a victim can never decide whether they are a victim or not.

Did Robert Lee Willie's execution, did it give you some peace?

Harvey: I know he won't kill again. I know there can't be another mother that comes to me and tells me he had a history of escaping from jail, you knew what he was like, why didn't you try to see that he got the sentence that was handed down and felt like I had to.

We Have to Speak for the Victims

Going back to the prison, as you do for other executions, why do you do that?

Harvey: I go to Angola when there's an execution up there and I stand at the front gates to support capital punishment because the victim cannot be there. This day we wouldn't be standing there if there hadn't been somebody inside that has decided themselves to commit that crime. And the victim cannot be there any longer. And the news media, our society doesn't remember any longer who that victim was. And I'm there representing that victim because they can't be there.

Tell me what you think of Sister Helen Prejean—her work and her views.

Harvey: Well, I try to get to know her. I thought that she has a lot of contacts out there with nuns. There's a lot of people that are victims throughout the United States and if you go to court to a murder trial, you'll see a lot more people there supporting the criminal side than you'll ever see supporting the victims. By that time all their support is gone and they're usually sitting there in the courtroom all by themselves. And I thought that the contacts she had she could—I thought nuns helped people in situations like that and stuff and that maybe there could be support out there for other ones—they've had no one. And I know I've been going to court and there was a mother there all by herself and no one there to support and that's something I don't believe that anybody should go through all alone. Especially when it was just an eight-year-old child, a little girl that was so brutally raped and killed and she was raped afterwards. And I wanted her to see the other side of the coin. I knew she did not know the other side of the coin. And that was what my whole outlook was and trying to be able for her to reach others that was victims, that there was help out there. But it didn't work out that way.

Do you feel in some way like she's judging you?

Harvey: I don't know whether Helen Prejean is judging me personally or not, but I know she has a goal and there's a lot of support. Helen Prejean is out for us to lose capital punishment. Her goal is that we have capital punishment here in the United States no longer. And I don't think that there is any way in this world that we can send the message out that only the people are going to speak up for people that have committed such a heinous crime, that we're going to work to try to see that you go on living. I think we have got to and the public better realize that if they do not speak up, they do not react, you know the victims have a voice no more. And if we don't speak for them, they are going to be silent forever. And we have got to speak up that no, we don't want our loved ones murdered. It isn't OK for you to go on living and kill our loved ones.

Three-quarters of the people as I understand it in the country are for capital punishment. Why do you think Sister Helen Prejean is getting so much attention?

Harvey: Because that's what the news media is doing. They've given her that attention. She couldn't have gotten it all by herself.

He Didn't Seem Sorry

What were Robert Lee Willie's last words to you?

Harvey: Well, I was sorry that we weren't allowed to speak on the Angola grounds. But he was brought in by the guards. And they had him underneath his arms if he had balked or his legs gave way. They brought him up to the mike and warden asked him did he have a last statement and he said, "All I have to say is Mr. and Mrs. Harvey I hope you get some satisfaction from my death, that killing is wrong. With this individual society nation the killing is wrong."

Did he mean it? Did he feel like he was apologizing to you?

Family and friends of murder victims gather in vigil outside a prison complex as an inmate is executed. AP/Wide World Photos

Harvey: He definitely didn't sound like he was apologizing. To me it sounded like words coming out of Helen Prejean's mouth and it was never any words was typed that would have come out Robert Lee Willie's mouth. And he didn't act like he was sorry for any of his crimes that he committed, much less the brutal murder of our daughter.

How did it make you feel, his punishment?

Harvey: I thought he got the sentence that he deserved. That he decided himself. He knew it was on the books. He chose to go ahead and murder her and I thought he deserved that sentence.

And when you learned what happened to Faith. . . .

Harvey: She was found at Frickie's Cave near Franklinton, Louisiana. And she was left there with her throat cut. She had been brutally raped and she fought for her life and had some fingers cut off. And she had been raped long after her death. It took us eight days to find her.

It took you eight days. . . .

Harvey: Could you forgive somebody that last minutes, hours, seconds, that was lived in the torture and the hell that an 18-year-old went through? Can you think of forgiving somebody for what all that her last hours on this earth was like? I don't think Faith ever did anything in her life to deserve an exit from this earth like that. It's nothing I ever imagined for her. She had too many plans. She was off to go into the service. She's off to serve her country. She was planning to do a lot of things with foreign language, she thought that there was an endless list of how she could help others and translating for them that were in trouble.

I Can't Forgive Him

And when people say that the proper punishment for those two was life imprisonment, what do you say?

Harvey: If they didn't commit the crime, they wouldn't have gotten the sentence. They didn't have to brutally murder her. They took her to rape her. And then they didn't want her to be able to identify them. And so they killed her the way that they did. But they didn't leave her there. They raped her long after her death. I think they gave up that right when they made those decisions.

It really frustrates me that people won't get out and voice their opinion and support the capital punishment. You know the victim's voice is silent forever and if we don't speak up for them, who is going to? Every right that they ever had on the face of this earth's been taken from them. And I don't think that there is another human being that has a right to decide your fate and take the one thing from you that is really yours—and that's your life. That you can't get back. If somebody steals your car, you can work harder and you can get another car but there's no way for you to work or do anything else in this world to get back your life. When it's gone, it's gone. And if people don't start voicing their support for capital punishment we're gonna lose it again. They think no we won't. Most of us are for the capital punishment. But look at history. 1972, we lost it.

Again, this question of forgiveness. . . . Could you have forgiven Robert Lee Willie for what he did to Faith?

Harvey: When he took the stand in the second sentencing phase of his trial, he admitted he was in between Faith's legs. In other words he admitted raping her. The first thing the coroner said to us that she could have never been saved because of the brutal rape. I couldn't have forgiven him for torturing her so. I don't think that—he was asked why didn't you try to get help for her? Why didn't you try to take her to the hospital? They told her—I told him how many miles it was to a hospital and all the world he cared for was about himself. And what he wanted to do. He was through. He had done his damage and he was ready to go and he wanted to get out of there. He just didn't want to be found there with the body. And that I can't forgive. He didn't care anything about her.

What do you think of when you go visit her gravesite?

Harvey: The love, the joy that I enjoyed with Faith. The time I'm thankful that I know where Faith is. That I know what I have buried there, what I don't have buried there. She brought a lot of joy in my life. Did you read that poem that my sister wrote? She meant a whole lot to our family and she was a lot of joy. And I miss that. I miss it a great deal.

Vengeance Is Not the Solution

Bud Welch

On April 19, 1995, the Alfred P. Murrah Federal Building was just beginning to bustle with the activities of the day when at 9:02 an explosion ripped through the building killing 168 people—19 of them children—and leaving hundreds of others injured. One of those killed was Julie Welch.

Julie's father, Bud Welch, wanted vengeance for bomber Timothy McVeigh. He was certain that he would only find relief when McVeigh was executed. But as the months wore on, Welch came to believe that the death penalty was based on rage and hate, the same motivations that had led to the bombing itself. He changed his position and began to argue against the death penalty for McVeigh. Despite his efforts, McVeigh was executed in 2001.

Bud Welch travels around the country speaking out against the death penalty. He is also on the board of directors of the organization Murder Victims' Families for Reconciliation.

There's Been Enough Bloodshed

When my only daughter, Julie, was killed, I joined a "club" that I wish had no members. The price of admission is too high. I know the pain of losing a loved one because of a senseless act of violence.

Julie Marie was the light of my life. She was so bright, so kind, and so caring. She was my friend and confidante. After graduating from college, Julie worked as a Spanish interpreter for the Social Security Administration in Oklahoma City. Every Wednesday, we met for lunch at a Greek restaurant across the street from the Murrah Federal Building. Our lunch date on Wednesday, April 19, 1995, was never to be.

Bud Welch, "Timothy McVeigh Killed My Daughter," *Why Forgive?* Farmington, PA: Plough Publishing House, 2000. Copyright © 2000 by Bud Welch. Reproduced by permission.

Julie spoke five languages and used her abilities to help disadvantaged people. On the morning of the bombing, she had gone into the lobby to meet her clients. Julie always did things like that. If she had stayed in her office instead of meeting the clients in the lobby, she would have survived.

I'm the third oldest of eight children, raised on a dairy farm in central Oklahoma. I've run a gasoline service station for 35 years. All my life, I had always opposed the death penalty. I had often been told over a cup of coffee with friends who supported the death penalty that if something ever happened to one of my family members, I would change my mind—"What if Julie was raped and murdered?"

I Was Filled with Rage

When Julie was killed that morning with 167 others in the bomb blast at the Murrah Building, the pain I felt was unbearable. I was also filled with rage. I wanted Timothy McVeigh executed. I could have done it with my bare hands. I didn't even want a trial. I just wanted him fried. I call it the "insanity period"—I went through five weeks of insanity. Now I know why people accused of committing horrible crimes are rushed from the car to the courthouse wearing bulletproof vests—because victims' family members are so crazed and angry that they would take the law into their own hands.

I remembered President [Bill] Clinton and Attorney General Janet Reno, while Julie's body was still missing, saying that they were going to seek and obtain the death penalty for the perpetrators. That sounded so wonderful to me at the time, because I had been crushed, and that was the big fix.

But I also remembered the time Julie and I were driving across Iowa during her junior year of college, listening to a newscast on the radio about an execution. Julie said, "Dad, what they're doing in Texas makes me sick. All they're doing is teaching hate to their children. It has no social redeeming value." I didn't think much about it at the time, but after Julie was killed, it kept echoing in my mind.

Nine months after the bombing, I was still stuck on April 19. I was drinking heavily and smoking three packs of cigarettes a day. One cold January day, I went down to the bomb site. I sat under the old elm tree where Julie used to park her car. I asked myself, "Once they're tried and executed, what then? How's that going to help me? It isn't going to bring Julie back." I asked myself that question for two weeks. I finally realized that the death penalty was nothing more than revenge and hate. And revenge and hate are exactly why Julie and 167 others are dead.

I Chose to Forgive

A few weeks after the bombing I saw Bill McVeigh, Tim's father, on television. He was working in his flowerbed. The reporter asked him a question, and when he looked into the television camera for a few seconds, I saw a deep pain in a father's eyes that most people could not have recognized. I could, because I was living that pain. And I knew that some day I had to go tell that man that I truly cared about how he felt.

One Saturday morning two years later, I finally found myself in Bill McVeigh's driveway. I sat in the car, not knowing what I was going to be able to say. Then I went up and knocked. He came to the door, and I introduced myself. I said, "I understand that you have a large garden in your backyard," and that excited him. He said, "Oh, yeah, would you like to see it?" I said, "I'd love to."

So, we spent the first half-hour in that garden getting to know one another. Then we went into the house, and spent an hour visiting at the kitchen table. His 23-year-old daughter Jennifer was there. As I walked in I noticed a photograph of Tim above the mantelpiece. I kept looking at it as we were sitting at the table. I knew that I had to comment on it at some point, so finally I looked at it and said, "God, what a good-looking kid." Bill said, "That's Tim's high school graduation picture." A big tear rolled out of his right eye, and at that moment I saw in a father's eyes a love for his son that was absolutely incredible.

After our visit I got up, and Jennifer came from the other end of the table and gave me a hug; we cried, and I held her face in my hands and told her, "Honey, the three of us are in this for the rest of our lives. And we can make the most of it if we choose. I don't want your brother to die. And I will do everything in my power to prevent it."

Driving back to Buffalo, I couldn't see through my glasses because I was still sobbing. When I got back I sat and sobbed and sobbed, and made a total ass out of myself for an hour. But I have never felt closer to God in my life than I did at that moment. It felt like a load had been taken completely off my shoulders. I wish I could make you understand the way it felt.

The Death Penalty Can Prevent Healing

All of my family members opposed Tim McVeigh being executed. The last one to come aboard was my mother, who was 88. Mom was very angry at me for speaking out against the death penalty for Tim McVeigh, because she wanted him dead. Finally, she called me on the phone one day. She said, "Well, Bud, I hope it goes well for you. You're right about the death penalty. I guess I have enough of my anger gone now that I can believe that we shouldn't kill him."

I was speaking in Seattle recently. A lady told me she had always supported the death penalty. Her husband had been murdered in 1981, in Florida, and the murderer had killed other people, too. She had supported the death penalty right up until the execution of her husband's killer. Then, a week after the execution, she started to get this creepy feeling.

This woman told me that when the murderer was alive, she could take her rage out on him. But once he was dead, she had nowhere to release the rage. The prosecutor never told her that she might go through this mental and emotional crisis once the guy was executed. She told me that if she knew then what she knows now, she would have done everything she could to stop that execution. I have heard that many times. So the death penalty can actually prevent healing, rather than helping.

Going Forward

The day after Julie's burial someone asked me about "closure." I can't stand that word. Of course I was still in hell then. In a way, I still am. How can there ever be true closure? A part of my heart is gone. Julie's death still grips me every single day. But I no longer carry that horrible vengeance and rage because it would destroy me.

Of course, forgiving is not something you wake up one morning and decide to do. I still have these moments of rage, when I think, "What am I doing? That bastard didn't deserve to live." You have to work through your anger and hatred as long as it's there. You try to live each day a little better than the one before.

There's been enough bloodshed. We don't need any more. To me the death penalty is vengeance, and vengeance doesn't really help anyone in the healing process. Of course, our first reaction is to strike back. But if we permit ourselves to think through our feelings, we might get to a different place.

Organizations to Contact

Amnesty International USA (AI)
5 Penn Plaza, New York, NY 10001
(212) 807-8400 • fax: (212) 627-1451
website: www.amnesty-usa.org

Amnesty International is an independent worldwide movement working for the release of all prisoners of conscience,
fair and prompt trials for political prisoners, and an end to
torture and executions. AI is funded by donations from its
members and supporters throughout the world. AI has published several books and reports, including *Fatal Flaws: Innocence and the Death Penalty.*

Canadian Coalition Against the Death Penalty (CCADP)
PO Box 38104, 550 Eglinton Ave. W
  Toronto, ON M5N 3A8
(416) 693-9112 • fax: (416) 686-1630
e-mail: ccadp@home.com
website: www.ccadp.org

CCADP is a not-for-profit international human rights organization dedicated to educating the public about alternatives to
the death penalty worldwide and to providing emotional and
practical support to death row inmates, their families, and the
families of murder victims. The center releases pamphlets and
periodic press releases, and its Web site includes a student resource center providing research information on capital punishment.

**Capital Punishment Project, American Civil Liberties
Union (ACLU)**
125 Broad St., 18th Fl., New York, NY 10004
(212) 549-2500 • fax: (212) 549-2646
website: www.aclu.org

The project is dedicated to abolishing the death penalty. The ACLU promotes the view that capital punishment violates the Constitution's ban on cruel and unusual punishment as well as the requirements of due process and equal protection under the law. It publishes and distributes numerous books and pamphlets, including *The Case Against the Death Penalty* and *Frequently Asked Questions Concerning the Writ of Habeas Corpus and the Death Penalty.*

Death Penalty Focus of California
870 Market St., Suite 859, San Francisco, CA 94102
(415) 243-0143 • fax: (415) 243-0994
e-mail: info@deathpenalty.org
website: www.deathpenalty.org

Death Penalty Focus of California is a nonprofit organization dedicated to the abolition of capital punishment through grassroots organization, research, and the dissemination of information about the death penalty and its alternatives. It publishes the quarterly newsletter the *Sentry.*

Death Penalty Information Center (DPIC)
1101 Vermont Ave. NW, Suite 701, Washington, DC 20005
(202) 289-2275 • fax: (202) 289-7336
e-mail: pbernstein@deathpenaltyinfo.org
website: www.deathpenaltyinfo.org

DPIC conducts research into public opinion on the death penalty. The center believes capital punishment is discriminatory and excessively costly and that it may result in the execution of innocent persons. It publishes numerous reports, such as *Millions Misspent: What Politicians Don't Say About the High Costs of the Death Penalty, Innocence and the Death Penalty: Assessing the Danger of Mistaken Executions,* and *With Justice for Few: The Growing Crisis in Death Penalty Representation.*

Justice Fellowship (JF)
44180 Riverside Pkwy., Lansdowne, VA   20176
(800) 217-2743 • fax: (800) 554-8579
website: www.justicefellowship.org

The fellowship is a Christian organization that bases its work for reform of the justice system on the concept of victim-offender reconciliation. It does not take a position on the death penalty, but it publishes the pamphlet *Capital Punishment: A Call to Dialogue.*

Justice for All (JFA)
PO Box 55159, Houston, TX   77255
(713) 935-9300 • fax: (713) 935-9301
e-mail: info@jfa.net
website: www.jfa.net

Justice for All is a not-for-profit criminal justice reform organization that supports the death penalty. Its activities include circulating online petitions to keep violent offenders from being paroled early and publishing the monthly newsletter *Voice of Justice.*

Lamp of Hope Project
PO Box 305, League City, TX   77574-0305
e-mail: aspanhel@airmail.net
website: www.lampofhope.org

The project was established and is run primarily by Texas death row inmates. It works for victim-offender reconciliation and for the protection of the civil rights of prisoners, particularly the right of habeas corpus appeal. It publishes and distributes the periodic *Texas Death Row Journal.*

Lincoln Institute for Research and Education
1001 Connecticut Ave. NW, Suite 1135
  Washington, DC   20036
(202) 223-5112

The institute is a conservative think tank that studies public policy issues affecting the lives of black Americans, including the issue of the death penalty, which it favors. It publishes the quarterly *Lincoln Review.*

National Coalition to Abolish the Death Penalty (NCADP)
1717 K St. NW, Suite 510, Washington, DC 20036
(202) 331-4090 • fax: (202) 331-4099
e-mail: info@ncadp.org
website: www.ncadp.org

The National Coalition to Abolish the Death Penalty is a collection of more than 115 groups working together to stop executions in the United States. The organization compiles statistics on the death penalty. To further its goal the coalition publishes *Legislative Action to Abolish the Death Penalty*, information packets, pamphlets, and research materials.

National Criminal Justice Reference Service (NCJRS)
U.S. Department of Justice, Rockville, MD 20849-6000
(301) 519-5500
e-mail: askncjrs@ncjrs.org
website: www.ncjrs.org

The National Criminal Justice Reference Service is one of the most extensive sources of information on criminal and juvenile justice in the world. For a nominal fee this clearinghouse provides topical searches and reading lists on many areas of criminal justice, including the death penalty. It publishes an annual report on capital punishment.

For Further Research

Books

Hugo Adam Bedau, *Debating the Death Penalty: Should America Have Capital Punishment? The Experts on Both Sides Make Their Case.* New York: Oxford University Press, 2005.

John Bessler, *Kiss of Death: America's Love Affair with the Death Penalty.* Boston: Northeastern University Press, 2003.

Antoinette Bosco, *Choosing Mercy: A Mother of Murder Victims Pleads to End the Death Penalty.* New York: Orbis, 2001.

Donald Cabana, *Death at Midnight: The Confession of an Executioner.* Boston: Northeastern University Press, 1996.

Tim Junkin, *Bloodsworth: The True Story of the First Death Row Inmate Exonerated by DNA.* New York: Algonquin, 2004.

Rachel King, *Capital Consequences: Families of the Condemned Tell Their Stories.* New Brunswick, NJ: Rutgers University Press, 2005.

———, *Don't Kill in Our Names: Families of Murder Victims Speak Out Against the Death Penalty.* New Brunswick, NJ: Rutgers University Press, 2003.

Evan J. Mandery, *Capital Punishment: A Balanced Examination.* Sudbury, MA: Jones & Bartlett, 2004.

Debbie Morris, *Forgiving the Dead Man Walking: Only One Woman Can Tell the Entire Story.* Grand Rapids, MI: Zondervan 2000.

Robert W. Murray, *Life on Death Row*. Bloomington, IN: Authorhouse, 2003.

Carroll Pickett, *Within These Walls: Memoirs of a Death House Chaplain*. New York: St. Martin's, 2002.

Helen Prejean, *Dead Man Walking*. New York: Vintage, 1994.

Richard M. Rossi, *Waiting to Die: Life on Death Row*. London: Vision Paperbacks, 2004.

Scott Sundby, *A Life and Death Decision: A Jury Weighs the Death Penalty*. New York: Palgrave Macmillan, 2005.

Scott Turow, *Ultimate Punishment: A Lawyer's Reflection on Dealing with the Death Penalty*. New York: Picador, 2004.

Nanon Williams, *Still Surviving*. Gardena, CA: Breakout, 2003.

Periodicals

Clay Conrad, "Death Qualification Leads to Biased Juries," *USA Today*, March 2001.

Thomas R. Eddlem, "Ten Anti–Death Penalty Fallacies," *New American*, June 3, 2002.

Sarah Brown Hammond, "Questioning Capital Punishment: DNA Has Been Used to Exonerate a Number of Death Row Inmates, Calling into Question the Reliability of the System," *State Legislatures*, September 2005.

Jennifer Hickey, "Dining with Capital Punishment," *Insight on the News*, May 28, 2001.

Christopher Hitchens, "Tinkering with the Death Machine," *Nation*, July 22, 2002.

Michael Hurd, "Long Live the Death Penalty," *Capitalism Magazine*, February 20, 2003.

Earl Ofari Hutchinson, "Searching for a Silver Lining in Death Penalty's Gender Bias," *Pacific News Service*, November 29, 2004.

David Kirby, "Was Justice Served?" *Advocate*, February 27, 2001.

Gerald F. Kreyche, "Death—the Final Frontier," *USA Today*, May 2002.

Robert Kuttner, "Life After Death," *American Prospect*, July 2004.

Tom Lowenstein, "The Last Face You'll Ever See: The Private Life of the American Death Penalty," *American Prospect*, December 3, 2001.

Karen Olsson, "Death Wish," *Boston Globe*, January 1, 2006.

Adam Caine Ortiz, "Juvenile Death Penalty: Is It Cruel and Unusual in Light of Contemporary Standards?" *Criminal Justice Magazine*, Winter 2003.

George Pataki, "The Death Penalty Is a Deterrent," *USA Today*, March 1997.

Mary Frances Robinson, "A Humane Death Sentence," *Humanist*, July 2000.

Victor Streib, "Moratorium on the Death Penalty," *Duke Law Journal*, Autumn 1998.

Christina Swarns, "The Uneven Scales of Capital Justice: How Race and Class Affect Who Ends Up on Death Row," *American Prospect*, July 2004.

———, "Juveniles and the Death Penalty," *Washington Times*, September 2, 2002.

Steve Weinberg, "The Wrong Man: A True Story of Innocence on Death Row," *Columbia Journalism Review*, September 2001.

Charles Whitaker, "The Death Penalty Debate: Are We Killing Innocent Black Men?" *Ebony*, May 1999.

Web Sites

The Clark County Prosecutor (www.clarkprosecutor.org). A comprehensive pro–death penalty Web site that offers opinions from both sides and more than one thousand death penalty links.

The Death Penalty (www.yesdeathpenalty.com). A pro–death penalty resource with links to opinions on the death penalty in other countries. It also offers the Web book *The Death Penalty: A Defense*, written by Dave Anderson.

The International Justice Project (www.internationaljusticeproject.org). Web site of an organization that favors abolishing the death penalty. It promotes increased application of international law and human rights standards to questions about capital punishment.

Pro Death Penalty (www.prodeathpenalty.com). A comprehensive resource on all aspects of the death penalty state by state.

Index